sex toys

A frank and fun
introduction to
the most popular
playthings you can buy

Lisa Sussman

CARLTON
BOOKS

Contents

Introduction

The world of sex toys can be more than a little mind-boggling. However, you've come to the right place to get all the answers. Whether you are a singleton and loving it or your "me" has merged into a "we", sex toys are a fabulous way to boost the pleasure quotient in your sex life.

If you've made it this far, you're obviously curious about sex toys. But still, you might be asking, why should I use a sex toy? My sex life is good/pretty good/great/glorious most of the time. Answer: why shouldn't you?

Sex toys have been around for thousands of years (see timeline below), so something about them must work. There are a million ways to enjoy these gadgets. Why not find out what you've been missing? And let's face it – the number one reason to buy a sex toy is for the intense and instant gratification that they deliver. There is such a large choice available that you can choose one custom-made to satisfy all of your sexual whims and needs.

As a sex writer, I know that there are far too many people in the world having far too few orgasms. Kinsey, the famous sex researcher, determined that 70 per cent of all women don't come to orgasm by penetration alone, and according to a University of Chicago survey, roughly 25 per cent of all women (compared to 8 per cent of all men) fail to have orgasms at all during sex. No wonder women need sex toys – to make up for such disappointments. (Or, perhaps, to add to the bedtime activities and ensure that those disappointments don't happen again.)

While using a sex toy won't necessarily keep you in perpetual "whoo-hoo" mode, (although I do know of one woman who disappeared to her room for two heavenly days after purchasing her first vibrator – a Pocket Rocket for the label-obsessed among you), they do put many a woman who has had trouble climaxing in the past on the inside big bang track. And, since one good explosion deserves another, this

Circa 500bc: Invention of an early version of the dildo in Greece. Made of wood or leather, they required liberal lubrication of olive oil for comfortable use.

Circa 300bc: The Kama Sutra makes the first mention of penis extenders, suggesting that they can be crafted from wood, leather, buffalo horn, copper, silver, ivory or gold.

AD500: Invention of the first Ben Wa balls.

1200: The first cock rings were being used in China (made from goats' eyelids).

1791: The Marquis de Sade (the word "sadism" comes from his name) publishes *Justine*, which popularized BDSM sex toys like riding crops, whips, nipple clips and restraining devices.

4

elastic and fantastically stronger and later leading to the development of rubber condoms, dildos and other sex toys.

1869: The first vibrator is invented, a steam-powered machine recommended for treatment of "hysteria".

1882: The first electro-mechanical vibrator appears – this is the great-grandparent of today's vibrators.

1890s: Motion pictures are invented and the first porn movies are produced showing women playing with vibrators and dildos, including strap-ons.

1899: The first advertisement for a home electric vibrator, the Vibratile, appears in America as a cure for headache, wrinkles, and "neuralgia", or nerve pain.

in turn has been discovered to have the marvellous knock-on effect of leading to a happier, more blissful life in general. That's right – studies show that happy horizontal equals happy vertical. While I won't go so far as to say that having an electronic orgasm will cure all your troubles, any orgasm had on a regular basis – whatever the means – will definitely make you feel more sexually open, expressive and confident and help you generally to like yourself and your life better.

Sex toys are empowering. They tell the world you are in charge of your own pleasure. Rather than just sitting at home, twiddling your thumbs and waiting for some man to figure out how to give you satisfaction, you are using those thumbs to control the on-off switch of your vibrating tube of joy and send yourself into spasms of ecstasy. Many women have already joyfully discovered this fact. Apparently, sex toys 'r' us. Around 20 per cent of women use a vibrator while masturbating. Thirty percent of strap-on sales are to couples.

And while many high-street stores are having trouble balancing their books, Ann Summers, purveyor of saucy toys and underwear in the UK, has seen its sales rise by as much as 65 per cent in the past few years. While the company is still not permitted to advertise its vacancies in job centres (being deemed a branch of the sex industry), buying a Rampant Rabbit (a pink plastic combo stimulator that is one of their biggest sellers) has become no more risqué than buying a pint of milk.

The other good news is that sex toys have come a long way from the early hand-mixer-shaped vibrators that looked like they would beat your clitoris to a pulp and made more noise than a Harley revving up, or repulsive pieces of rubber resembling a 30cm (12 inch) long hotdog. Today's savvy shopper will find a huge array of discreet, easy-to-use doo-dahs. The beauty of these toys is their amazing versatility – virtually all can be used alone or with a partner, many have adjustable settings so you have complete control, and they're small enough so that no one

1907: The Penis Stiffener, a hollow, metal cylinder with a wide opening at one end for insertion of the penis and a small opening at the other to allow sperm into the vagina, wins a US patent for helping men with erection problems.

1927: KY Jelly hits the scene.

1930: Latex rubber – lighter, softer and more pliable than its vulcanized cousin – is invented.

1953: Debut of *Playboy* magazine (men bought it just for the articles).

1998: The Rabbit vibrator makes an appearance on *Sex and the City*.

2000: Sex-toy parties become a popular way to shop.

6

will suspect that that's not a Palm Pilot in your pocket. Some do everything a penis can't and others work best when used with a partner.

Then there are the sex-ed salons. Large groups of screaming women passing dildos between their legs may sound like a scene straight out of a porno movie, but it is actually a sight that is becoming more and more common in suburban homes worldwide. The basic idea behind these so-called "pleasure parties" is the same as a Tupperware or Avon party of old: a saleswoman comes to someone's home and presents and demonstrates merchandise to a group of friends, which is then available for purchase after the party. The difference here is that instead of lipsticks and nail polish being served up with your drinks and crisps, your friendly neighbourhood "schtupperware" party offers the latest models of sex toys, which may include discreet vibrators disguised to look like lipstick and nail-polish bottles! And if you think this is

getting too down and dirty, well, the NHS is giving out vibrators in some districts to women who have trouble climaxing.

In the following pages, I am going to describe the most popular sex toys out there, why you should try them and how to use them. There are models designed to suit literally every occasion; from getting a non-alcohol related buzz at your cousin's wedding (there has to be some bonus for being forced to wear that hideous Bo-Peep frock), to making waves in the bath with a simple little waterproof ducky number. You can get a vibrator to match your iMac or a cock ring that looks like a bow tie. There are even props to transform you into Xena, Warrior Princess or help you to make your own Tie Her Up, Tie Her Down scenario.

Before too long, you may even be ready to adopt my mantra:

"She who dies with the most toys, wins!"

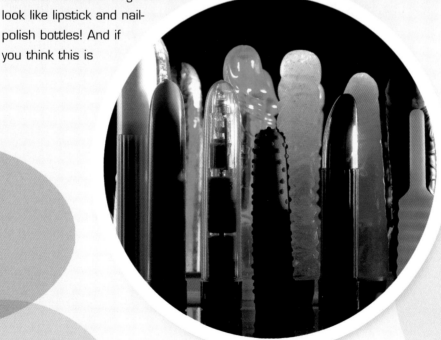

part one

Getting Started

Just like when you are choosing lovers, you should be selective about choosing a sex toy. As with men, there is the right toy out there for every woman. In fact, there are several.

This section covers everything you need to know about getting started on shopping for your toy chest, from figuring out must-have playthings geared for your erotic appetite, to getting the knowledge on how to share your toys with others, as well as their general care and feeding so they keep on ticking and don't become a hazard to your health.

And, just in case you're still not completely sure that you're ready to become a babe in toyland, here are 13 reasons why you should make a play date with a sex aid right now:

1 It's powered either by you, battery or electricity so, barring two broken hands, batteries being out of stock at your corner shop or a power cut, your toy will always be ready for action and can perform all night every night until you are totally, completely and 100 per cent satisfied.

2 You get to choose the size and shape so it will definitely be long enough and thick enough to please you.

3 You will almost definitely have an orgasm – even if you've never had one before.

4 Most women need lots of persistent, unrelenting clitoral stimulation to reach orgasm. Your friendly neighbourhood vibrator provides just that. Few men do.

5 If your sex life has become a little stale, sex toys will definitely freshen it up.

6 Sex toys don't break your heart and never fall asleep on you.

7 You get to experience lots of different and delicious stimulation, leading to lots of different and delicious types of orgasms and new levels of pleasure.

8 Did I mention guaranteed orgasm?

9 A sex toy gives the user complete control over the source of their pleasure, which in turn delivers the ultimate in sexual satisfaction.

10 If he's too quick, big, small, soft or tired for you, you can still have fun.

11 If you're in the mood and he isn't (or vice versa), it's no problem.

12 You may find new hot spots on your body (or his) you didn't know about.

13 Oh yeah, you'll have an amazing orgasm.

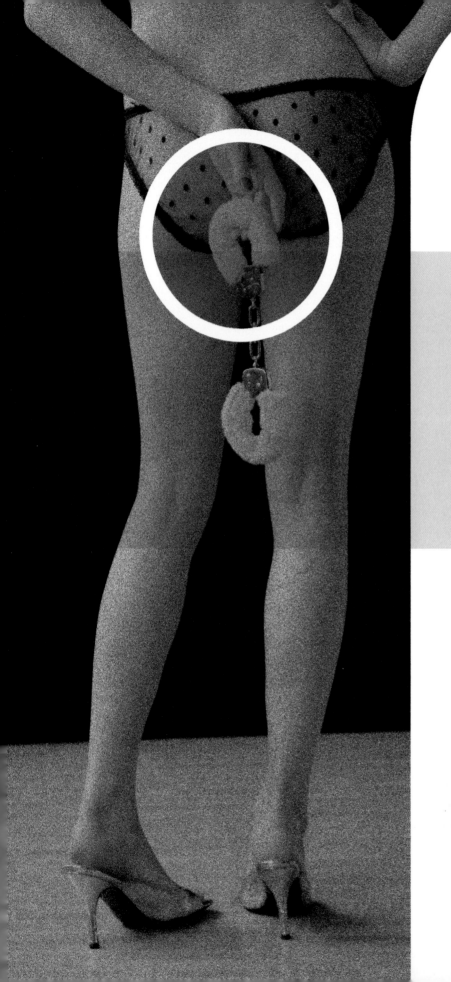

CHAPTER 1
getting into gear

- •BULLETS
- •BEADS
- •BUNNIES
- •BONDAGE

Take a wander through your neighbourhood **EROTICA SHOP** and overwhelm your mind (and later, your body). **Think X-rated buffet table.** There is something for every taste and occasion. You'll find **every shape, size and substance** imaginable (and some not so imaginable – **DOLPHIN SHAPED VIBRATOR** anyone? Just hum, "They call him Flipper"!).

Where to start? It's easy to think that not only will you never figure out how to choose the right sex toy to electrify your love life, you may literally shock yourself and end up taking a trip to accident and emergency instead of seventh heaven. Not to worry. Toys bought from well-known suppliers (see Resources) are safe as long as they are used correctly.

That said, you probably don't want to blow your pay cheque on a trial run. If you're a vibrator virgin, your best bet is to try a few less expensive toys to see where your tastes lie. Also check the returns policy where you buy. Better sex toy suppliers will let you return merchandise up to a certain point (usually 60 days) for any reason – even if you just decide you don't like it. Don't worry – the toys don't get resold!

Read on for the joys of toys: a primer for your pleasure. Check out the glossary at the back to get to grips with sex toy lingo.

For the buyer who would prefer a bit less face2face contact or doesn't live in a city where there are such shops, there are many mail order and online stores more than willing to send your goods in a plain box marked "NOT from www. sextoys.com". Actually, these stores are used to being discreet and generally keep their word. However, since you are required to give your address when buying from anywhere for delivery via post, make sure the store actually exists (see Resources for virtual and actual reputable shops) or you may find your details have been sold to other sex-related mailing lists – sort of negating the whole idea of not doing it in person in the first place.

Another place to buy is at special at-home get-togethers of friends and friends of friends. In the UK Ann Summers helps you book parties (see Resources) or you can go à la carte, getting together some sample goody bags, a group of gal pals and a pitcher of Cosmopolitans.

Shop 'til you drop

I know what you're thinking: You're going to walk into an "adult" store and all the shop girls (or worse – boys!) will be leeringly interested in you and your sexual tastes. Think again. Most clerks who sell remote-control vibrators are no more interested in you personally than the person who rings up your weekly veggie shop. But if you want to avoid your typical male-oriented porno-sleaze shop – and who wouldn't? – try one of the women-friendly sex-toy boutiques (see Resources). Often owned by women, they feature a large selection of products designed for female pleasure and usually strive to create a welcoming atmosphere where women (and couples) will feel comfortable.

vibrate for your health!

Once upon a time, not too long ago, doctors were giving women orgasms to keep them in the pink.

In the 1800s, women suffered from so-called "hysteria". Symptoms included irritability, anxiety and irrationality. Sounds like a bad case of PMT, doesn't it? Another condition was called "pelvic hyperaemia" – or congestion of the genitalia.

All these symptoms were relieved (not cured, mind you) by a simple visit to the family doc who routinely performed "vulvular massage" using an assortment of large steam-powered vibrators (devices the size of ground-to-air rocket launchers) until the woman reached an orgasm (called "hysterical paroxysm" at the time) to relieve the tension.

Once they were electrified, vibrators were marketed directly to women as home appliances. In fact, in a fine example of economic supply and demand, the vibrator was only the fifth household device to be electrified, after the sewing machine, fan, tea kettle and toaster! They were advertised in magazines as helping women feel "healthy, revitalized and refreshed" (pretty much the way you feel after having an orgasm, no?).

12 things you think about sex toys that are wrong, wrong, wrong!

1 I'll become addicted to it! While you may feel tempted to disappear with your new power tool for a few hours or even days at a time, there is actually no physiological basis for sex-toy addiction in the way that there is for, say, alcohol or cigarettes.

Bottom line: There is no wrong or right way to how you experience pleasure or how much pleasure you experience. You don't feel guilty when you listen to the same CD over and over. So why feel guilty if you use the same sex toy over and over? The key is to keep it varied. So if you are using your sex toy to the point where you're not really trying anything else, then all you need to do is put it away for a while (you will not go through withdrawal) and you'll soon be turning on to your lover's body again.

2 I won't want the real thing any more. What? You're worried that your new toy will feel so incredibly fabulous that you're actually going to like it too much and won't be able to come any other way? Think: sure, your toy only stops when you do ... but can it cuddle up to you at night, caress your back just the way you like, or kiss you so passionately it sends chills down your spine?

Now switch "sex toy" in that sentence with any other phrase: "If I try chocolate chip cookies, I'm afraid I'll like them so much I won't want to eat any other food." Or, "I'm afraid if I read a detective novel, I won't ever want to read a romance." Doesn't quite pack the same punch, does it?

There's a reason sex therapists give the thumbs up to sex toys: they're an ideal way to learn what stimulation your body responds to. A sex toy is only one out of thousands of delicious ways to enrich sexual play; it's not a substitute.

3 Sex toys are unnatural. No; eating a fast food burger that has been made from a genetically-modified and flavour-enhanced beef is unnatural. But using a sex toy to boost your love play is no more unnatural than lighting a candle, slipping into a sexy teddy, listening to romantic music or sending X-rated emails to your lover. Think about it: do the men who read *Playboy* worry about giving up real flesh-and-blood women (though we may worry for them!) or that they are in any way one orgasm shy of being sexually-depraved?

Think of sex products in the same spirit. They may not be something you want to use every single time you get naked, but they're still potentially useful, extremely convenient and quite delightful gadgets that are specifically designed for getting yourself off or enhancing your sighs when you romp with your partner. And you never know what you're missing until you've tried it. Something as simple as a bottle of olive oil mixed with a little peppermint essential oil can expand your sex goddess repertoire (and reputation) in a way you may never have imagined.

The operative word here, girls, is TOYS!

4 **Sex toys are only for losers.** The fact is that there are millions of women using sex toys, and they can't all be using them because they hate men/are single/ ugly/ lonely/ sexual deviants / desperate / dissatisfied with a man/can't get a man. They use them because they feel good.

5 **If I use a _____ people will think I'm _____:**
  - **vibrator/inadequate**
  - **butt plug /a freak**
  - **dildo/a dyke**
  - **restraint/a dominatrix**

Get over it. And I suppose if you're single, you must be desperate to be in a relationship?

Using a sex toy – whichever one you use – means one thing: you're taking charge of your sexuality. If it feels good and doesn't hurt you or anyone else, then go for it!

6 **SEX toys are only for hen parties or wannabe porn stars.** The fact that worldwide people spent over £1 billion on sex toys alone last year suggests that either we're all budding glamour models or there are a lot of people getting married. Chances are, your neighbour, your doctor, that cute guy at the coffee shop, your boss, even your parents have used/do use/will use sex toys. Join the party.

7 **Sex toys are only for masturbation.** While sex toys can certainly be used for a DIY orgasm, sex toys are no more only for masturbation than your sneakers are only for working out. Think multipurpose tool.

8 **If you have a solid relationship, there is no reason why you should need a sex toy.** Au contraire. Playing with sex toys can really make a good relationship even better. Using toys with your partner can actually make your relationship stronger because it shows that you two have good communication, trust each other, are comfortable and intimate enough to be able to try new things together, know how to have a laugh together, are determined not to let your sex life get stale and want to give each other great orgasms.

9 **I already have great orgasms, so I don't need a sex toy.** Aren't we all just thrilled for you. However, sex toys are specifically designed to give you pleasure. A quick example: the clitoris has 8,000 nerves in it. A vibrator will supply constant stimulation to those nerves that a hand or tongue simply cannot provide adequately. Just think of how that pressure might intensify your already fulfilling orgasm.

10 **I heard that sex toys are dangerous!** Honey, sex is dangerous. You're at risk of everything from genital warts to infertility whether you use protection or not when you sleep with someone who has not been given a clean bill of health.

Sex toys, on the other hand, are about as dangerous as using an electric can opener – all you need is common sense. Never use anything that is not marked waterproof near water. Keep your toys clean (see Chapter 4). And never use your vibrating pen in a meeting at work.

11 **I heard using a vibrator all the time can make you numb down there.** Just the opposite, actually. Some women heighten their sensation by using vibrators because they learn about the different sensations they like. From there, it's a short hop, skip and a jump to more – and sometimes more intense – orgasms.

12 **Buying toys would be just too humiliating** OK, I'll give you this one. In the beginning, it CAN be embarrassing to walk into a sex shop and pick out some toys. Which is why you don't have to (see Resources).

And now the truth – or rather, three truths:

1 **Sex toys feel good** – that is, unless you don't like the all-over-warm-tingly-drippy-starry sensation a really good orgasm gives you.

2 **Sex toys are good for you** – many women who have trouble reaching bliss or have never made it at all find that a sex toy (usually a vibrator) is just what they need to nudge them over the edge. Sex toys also increase your awareness of what turns your body on and help maintain great vaginal tone (great for keeping a firm grip on him).

3 **Sex toys are fun** – most couples get bored with vanilla sex. Using a toy can add a bit of flavour to your repertoire and add just enough "oomph" to turn a pretty good sexual experience into an outstanding one.

THE DIRTY DOZEN

Pick and choose from the following must-haves for your goodie box. While the colour, texture and exact style of toy that you choose are all personal choices (for instance, you may have an intense hatred of anything resembling a cuddly teddy bear – as one remote-controlled vibrator does), the following are good basic products to get you started to help you explore a range of sexual activities.

1   **Some sort of lubrication** (see Chapter 3).
2   **A vibrator:** these are as indispensable as your little black dress, once you are turned on to them. It's probably better to start "small" both in size and intensity since you can always upgrade later (check out Chapter 5 for the specifics of getting a buzz on). The best on show are:

*   **One of the rabbit styles:** these do it all. They provide powerful, multi-speed and stimulation, are easy to hold and very cute – what more could a girl want?

*   **Pocket rocket:** a little powerhouse – while no good for vaginal penetration, these are good, sturdy, multi-speed vibrators that are reliable.

*   **Finger vibrator:** thanks to the miracle of the watch battery, you can now turn your finger into a vibrating powerhouse that goes wherever you want it to. This toy is great for those who prefer the skin-to-skin feel during masturbation, but who could use the extra buzz. And if it's a "Not tonight, dear, I have a headache" moment, you can use the vibrator to massage away the pain.

Work slowly with your new toy – you might find it's not the right shape or size. Sexperiment until you find the one that suits you.

- **Strap-on bullet:** you leave your hands free so you can busy yourself with exploring other areas.

- **Remote control:** this type of vibrator is most loved by couples. Combining all the best aspects of a strap-on with the action remote controlled, these vibrators pack vibrations powerful enough for pleasing you wherever you are.

3 **G-spot dildo** (see Chapter 6 for more on Dildos): just the ticket for helping you tickle your G-spot.

4 **Soft tampons** by Joy Division: you wouldn't expect to find menstrual products on a top sex toy list, but these babies are designed to allow comfortable and hygienic lovemaking – including oral action – during your period. They're very comfortable and barely noticeable during sex. Made of very squishy foam which expands to suit your shape when inside, they're a bit bigger than your average tampon – about 5cm (2 inches) across and 3.5cm (1.3 inches) deep – and have no string (which means only you need to know if you're wearing one).

5 **Scarves or some restraint device:** being tied up during sex is one of the simplest and cheapest ways to upgrade your meat-and-two-veg sexual experience (see Part Four for more on bondage lite).

6 **Feathers:** they tickle, tantalize and titillate and can double as a fabulous fashion accessory (think feather boa or earrings) or a room decoration (stick a few peacock feathers in a vase, handy for when you want to seduce him on the couch).

7 **Massage oil:** simple, sensuous, sexy and as within reach as that bottle of olive oil in your kitchen cupboard.

8 **Erotica:** because this is something you can easily do solo or with a companion, erotica is fabulous for turning yourself on and introducing a lover to the wide world of sex toys. It could be a sexy book, a triple-X flick or a hot website you log on to (see Resources for suggestions).

9 **Cock ring with clitoris stimulator:** these rings grasp him with the extra boost of massaging your love button at the same time. They come low-tech or battery operated (see Chapter 8 for more on cock rings).

10 **Vibrator extras:** dress according to your mood by accessorizing your power tool with a G-spot vibrator or a clit stimulator or any of the other extra vibrator add-ons available (see Chapter 5 for more).

11 **An anal toy:** this may seem too much like unknown territory but the bottom is seething with sensitive nerves, which are just crying out to be loved. Start small with a vibrator specifically made for anal play (see Chapters 5 and 10) or anal beads (see Chapter 10).

12 **Lastly ...** always remember to stock up on whatever batteries your toys use. Batteries tend to die quite quickly in sex toys, and you don't want to use the batteries from the smoke detector lest you leave the candles burning all night (try explaining that one to a fireman). Also, the one thing you can be sure of is that if a toy is going to run out of power, it will do so just before you reach orgasm.

Put your toys away

You are going to want to keep your toys within easy reach. In general, the nightstand is best. However, if you have a nosy flatmate or children, you may want something a bit more hard-to-discover.

You could try a high shelf in your closet. But think about how much fun it is going to be searching for it in the middle of a love session (one option is to stick on a couple of glow-in-the-dark stars so you can easily find it without turning on the light).

One clever option is to put them in something so obvious that no one would think to rummage through it: a shoebox, a sock drawer or small carry-on case are all possibilities. You could also slip your favourite toy or toy du jour between the mattress and box spring (but be careful of energetic romps that could break them). Inside an extra pillow on the bed also works.

For those really desperate for privacy, there's the Hide-Your-Vibe Pillow (available from most sex boutiques – see Resources).

There are many budget sampler kits available with a little of everything on your wish list, from a standard vibrator and a high-tech penis ring to a vibrating penis/clitoral stimulator, a multi-speed controller with an interchangeable attachment jack, a vibrating anal egg and even batteries.

One more item for those not in an exclusive relationship that has gone through the mandatory six-month STI screenings: condoms. The raincoat of choice is currently the pouchy condom. Unlike typical condoms that get tighter at the head, these get baggier, which gives the penis more room to move and creates friction that makes it more of a tingly experience for him. The condom targets the head of the penis because it is the most sensitive part. With less restriction at the head of the penis, he can pretend that he's not wearing a condom at all. Pleasure Plus is the original and it has little nubs inside the tip to further enhance sensation. In Spiral, the new kid on the block, features a spiralling pouch.

18

5 last answers to those questions you have about what sex toys to buy but are afraid to ask

1 I bought a butt plug but it does nothing for me

If at first you don't succeed, try, try again. Sex toys are not one size fits all (otherwise there would be no need for this book). And unfortunately, some are more hype than hallelujah! Which is why you need to read this book before buying – no skipping pages!

Think of it in the same way as buying any appliance – you research before opening up your wallet. Even then, you may need to test drive a few models before finding the one that makes your eyes roll in ecstasy. And even if it turns out that a butt plug is not your thing, you may discover that a Magic Wand vibrator is.

2 Will I be stopped by airport security if I travel with my vibrator?

Not if you think ahead when you pack. Since every piece of luggage is X-rayed and sometimes hand-searched, consider whether your toy looks like it could be used as a weapon (as some larger dual-action vibes and men's toys can). Even a full-sized bottle of lubricant or a toy cleaner could be mistaken for something less innocent.

In Japan, it's illegal to manufacture objects that resemble an anatomically-correct organ – hence vibrators shaped like rabbits, cats, dolphins and other wildlife.

Here are a few rules to travel by:

- Don't stash your toys in your hand luggage as this is where you are most likely to be flagged by security – especially if you look at all nervous.
- Pack batteries separately as airport security keeps an eye out for battery-powered objects. Removing the batteries also ensures that your suitcase won't suddenly start vibrating on the baggage pick-up.
- Stick with small and discreet items that don't scream sex toys (so leave your collection of realistic dildos at home).

Remember – anything metal will be picked up by security (like balls – see Chapter 8, p.89, for more on these toys). If – the horror! – your luggage is selected for closer inspection, don't freak out. Security staff have seen it all – they may even ask you if you're carrying anything potentially embarrassing (not that that will make it any easier to admit that you have a ten-speed vibrator in your bag). At any rate, chances are they won't make a big deal of the contents. If they do, remind yourself: they're jealous because you're so cool about exploring your sexuality.

PACK IT IN

Match your toy to your trip.

- **Beach Vacation:** pack a waterproof toy.
- **Romantic getaway:** stick with the more sensuous items. Try a travel collection as you'll get a little bit of everything without having to lug full-sized bottles of oils or edible treats around.
- **Family getaway:** opt for a discreet vibrator shaped like a pen, lipstick or keychain
- **Business trip:** since there's not usually a lot of downtime, bring something small and discreet so that you can just whip it out of your bag or briefcase at a moment's notice.

3 Do I have to get a new toy with each new lover? If your toy is made of a non-absorbent material such as silicone, acrylic, glass, or hard plastic, then only if you haven't been washing behind your toy's ears (see Chapter 4). Lose any toy made of latex, jelly, or Cyberskin™ as they're not meant for sharing.

However, some people are squeamish and don't want to think that the last time you used your anal plug was when you were viewing the hairy derrière of your ex. So no trips down memory lane and if he asks … don't tell.

4 Is there really any difference between an expensive love toy and one that costs one-fifth of the price?
This is a case of you get what you pay for. There is a lot of rubbish on the market. The cheap stuff doesn't last as long, doesn't feel as good and doesn't have as many pleasure features as the premium stuff. Think surrounding yourself in satin versus wrapping yourself in sandpaper. Which would you choose?

Generally, the cheaper materials tend to be plastic while the platinum grades are silicone, lifelike materials like Cyberskin™ and Futurotic®, and acrylic (see Material Girl p.23 for more on this).

Better toys also tend not to burn through their battery pack as quickly as cheaper versions, meaning you won't suddenly be left high and dry mid-passion. Premium massage oils have a better scent, leave fewer residues, taste better and do good things to your skin as well as your orgasms.

Lastly, the more a toy does for you, the more you will have to pay for it. For a bit more cash, you get extras like multi-speed, waterproof materials, rotating heads and beads and pulsing vibration patterns – all of which add to your pleasure.

Be careful if you are travelling to Texas, USA. There, dildos can be bought and sold only for entertainment value. Stores even have you sign a release form confirming your honourable intentions and stating that you will not be explaining how to use dildos to anyone.

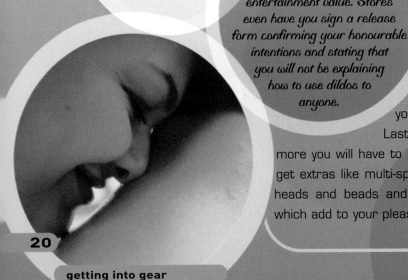

5 **Can I use a sex toy if I'm pregnant?** As long as everything is healthy and as it should be with your little bun (no bleeding, no placenta previa, no preterm labour, no cervical changes, no history of infections during pregnancy, no existing condition for which your doctor has recommended you abstain from sex), then there is no reason you can't have fun with your toy. Just be careful not to insert anything too deeply or forcefully into the vagina.

TOOLS OF THE TRADE
A harness is needed to hold a dildo in place when you must thrust

	YAY	NAY	BOTTOM LINE
LEATHER	Very strong, buttery (getting even softer with age) and form fitting; basic black is the popular colour (very slimming). Well-treated leather can last for years and years (some are guaranteed for life). Popular with fetishists.	Hard to clean, not waterproof, and you need to recondition the leather after cleansing to avoid cracking it.	Unless you're a hardcore vegan, leather just feels better!
WEBBING/NYLON/ELASTIC	The easiest of all harness materials to clean. You can throw it in the washing machine with your clothes without damaging it and then let it hang dry. It's less expensive than leather and fairly flexible. Plus it's water-safe.	A bit more limited than leather in a few ways: the padding is neoprene, a neat material that lasts for a long time, but the straps are like backpack straps and can dig into you.	Pretty much does everything as long as you can handle it.
RUBBER	Another material *du jour* for fetishists (they have all the fun), usually available in underwear styles.	After a few wears, they stretch, thin out and ultimately rip.	Can pong if not cleaned properly. Only for your Catwoman moments.
FABRIC	You can wash and wear it.	Not that reliable because it can't hold the weight of a dildo.	There really is no reason to invest in this.

21

GLASS

METAL

MATERIAL GIRL

A toy is useless to you if its material doesn't feel good

THE GOOD

GLASS

Super-slick and super-hard, gives a lot of pressure with almost no friction when it's lubed up; warms to your body and comes in some spectacularly beautiful shapes and colours; not porous, so easy to clean.

METAL

Largely enjoyed by S&M enthusiasts, can be sleek, cool and quite beautiful.

THE BAD

GLASS

Needs to be lubed to be comfortable but you need to be extra careful as the smoothness and slickness that make it ideal as a sex toy also make it slippery (and even more slippery when wet) and this leads to risk of breaking. The idea of using glass can be a bit scary to some. Keep it well away from hard surfaces – so no passionate scenes on the cement floor of your office warehouse.

METAL

Definitely not starter toys. Unlike the other materials, metal doesn't have any give to it at all.

THE UGLY

GLASS

Glass breaks fairly easily, and broken glass is very, very sharp. Even a small nick in a glass dildo will turn it immediately from a fun and useable sex toy into a razor-sharp tetanus-wand that you never, ever, ever want to get near your tender bits.

METAL

Go slowly. A sudden tap of a metal dildo against the pubic bone or cervix will hurt – a lot. Plus it can be just a bit too tinny to be sexy.

TITBIT

GLASS

Don't use a glass toy that isn't specifically intended to be used as a sex toy. Soda bottles, test tubes, light bulbs, etc. aren't smooth or strong enough for sex.

METAL

Plastic gives the same feel as metal without the risks.

22

SILICONE

REALISTIC & LIFELIKE
(Cyberskin™, Futurotic, Technoskin, UR3 etc)

Handcrafted, hypoallergenic completely non-porous so it's easy to clean, smooth to the touch; lasts forever; extremely soft and supple with a realistic feel that makes for an incredibly sensual experience; warms very nicely and quickly to your body temperature.

Warm to the touch and feel as similar to skin as you can get, softer than silicone or rubber, more sensual than jelly, very flexible, often handcrafted.

Can't be used with a silicone lubricant (See Chapter 3); pricey because it's handcrafted.

Some of the toys can be a bit too – er – realistic in look and feel, making you feel like Lorena Bobbit.

Silicone toys can tear easily if just a small crack has formed, so be careful not to break the surface.

They're often a little harder to care for – they need to be absolutely airtight and dry between use (see Chapters 3 and 4).

Though related, there is an important difference between silicone breast implants and silicone sex toys. The material in breast implants is a liquid silicone with loose molecules, which can penetrate into the blood stream if they leak. In silicone toys, the material is processed so that the molecules form a solid, though flexible, structure which cannot leak.

If you notice dark spots on your toy, throw it out – mould grows easily on realistics.

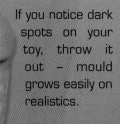

23

MATERIAL GIRL

THE STUFF

ACRYLIC

JELLY

THE GOOD

Seamless hard toys that can generally be heated or chilled for extra sensations; affordable; durable; quick to clean up; easy to mould so it can be formed into practically any shape; looks cool with its crystal-clear appearance – most could be left out and no one would be any the wiser.

Made of a soft, squishy plastic called polyvinyl chloride – PVC or the stuff plumbing pipes are made of; cheap and easy to work with and care for (it's the preferred material of most large sex toy manufacturers); flexible enough to bend to your body's curves; has good friction for thrusting motions (is often textured with ridges and nubs); quiet; rugged; cheap and colourful.

THE BAD

Can be a bit too hard and cold, it's fairly easy to do cosmetic damage to it (ruining its transparency and generally making it look a lot less cool)

The texture can be rubbery so needs to be used with a water-based lube.

THE UGLY

Highly flammable so no candle-lit moments.

Has a slightly off-putting rubbery odour – a cross between Vaseline and an inner tube.

TITBIT

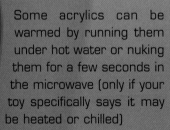

Some acrylics can be warmed by running them under hot water or nuking them for a few seconds in the microwave (only if your toy specifically says it may be heated or chilled)

Jelly is sold under a variety of names, including jel-lee, gelly, gel-lee, gellie and even MarbleGel. It's all the same stuff.

24

PLASTIC

LATEX

Among the least likely to absorb body fluids or react with your skin; hard and cool. Plastic vibrators can be very intense

Cheap, flexible but firm – which makes it ideal for first timers; extremely easy to clean; comes in a rainbow of colours.

Can be too hard and cool and the vibrations too intense; not realistic or soft. because they are smooth, vaginal or anal play can be a frictionless, dull affair.

Very porous so not as durable, especially if it isn't kept clean, and more likely to wear out.

Plastic vibrators can sound like a motorcycle revving up.

Some people may be allergic to latex – and only find out after they use it and have a reaction.

These are the toys you are most likely to see in a porn film (FYI: the veneer of choice tends to be silver).

Cover it up with a condom to be safe.

CHAPTER 2
pleased to meet you

SEX is hard to **talk** about – harder to talk about than love, in fact. Which is why most of our **SEXUAL VOCABULARY** consists of three words: **"Mmm"**, **"Uh huh"** – and when the going gets good – **"OHMIGOD!"**.

No wonder the prospect of bringing up using sex toys with your partner can seem more difficult than climbing Everest. Part of the problem is the words themselves – saying things like "sexual aids" or "sex toys" can make you feel like a sad sex-starved loser who needs help in the nookie department (call the emergency services now). Resorting to the name of specific toys – vibrator, cock ring, anal beads, handcuffs, dildo; basically, the whole sex paraphernalia shebang – can make you sound like you're auditioning for a porn movie.

And then there are the biggies that talking about sex toys brings on: shame; embarrassment; fear that your partner will be shocked by what you think are your less-than-orthodox sexual tastes, or will think that you are somehow looking to replace the man in your life with a vibrating bunny pal who only runs out when his batteries do. After all, shouldn't your lover's body (and your own) be enough? Would you need these things if you had your sorry sex act together?

Besides, if this is about love, shouldn't your partner be able to sense, wordlessly, what your body craves? (In romantic novels, the pirate king never has to be told how to tune into the maiden's deepest, darkest desires … he just knows). Shouldn't he just come home and plonk a Magic Wand on the table with a sexy leer?

But men are not mind readers. Nor are they easily traumatized (they are, after all, the same gender that can eat and pee at the same time). And the fact is the average guy is often so worried about making sure you have an orgasm that, if approached with tact, he'll be delighted by some outside support.

Here are some scenarios to use to talk yourself into a better sex life.

9

things you should do with a guy before you introduce him to your vibrator THING

The more of the following you manage, the easier it will be to get him to share your toys.

1. Exchange names – first, middle, last, embarrassing childhood nicknames, the works.

2. Have the sexual history talk. Yes, you have to.

3. Have sex at least once.

4. Swap dirty jokes (if it feels too dirty, how do you think he's going to react when you say, "butt plug"?)

5. Try everything you can to have an orgasm with him at least once (in other words, give him all the non-verbal cues – move his hands, shift your body – or even use actual words and talk to him about what turns you on).

6. Tell him a secret – and keep a secret he's told you.

7. Stay in bed with him all day.

8. Experience one disastrous sex moment – maybe he can't rise to the occasion or the condom gets lost inside of you – and come out laughing.

9. Window-shopped sex toys. You don't have to actually peruse the shelves of a sex boutique, but the phrase, "sex toys" should at least pass your lips and you should duly note his reaction. As in: you're passing a sex-toy store or come across a sex toy catalogue and you casually ask, **"Hmm, sex toys. What do you think of them?"**

MAKE A PLAY DATE WITH YOUR PARTNER

If you lose the power of speech when it comes to bringing up sex toys, here's a two-step approach to dropping a hint he can't miss.

STEP ONE
If you're shy:

♥ Test the waters with a little fantasy talk: the next time you're snuggling in bed, ask him what his top sexual fantasy is – and even if it involves you, a dog and his sister, don't freak out. A fantasy is the carte blanche of sexual communication: you can say what you want, but don't need to follow through unless you want to. All you are doing is planting a thought in his mind: sex toys.

So when it's your turn to tell all, mention that you fantasize about getting off with a sex toy and him. Get as graphic as you like or keep it lite. Then you can say, "Have you ever thought about something similar?"

If he says yes, that's a big green light. Proceed.

If he says no, no harm done. All he's saying is that he hasn't fantasized about it. The point is you have now put the subject on the page. You can temporarily end the conversation and then pick it up a few days later with, "Remember how we were talking about sex toys the other day? I read this article on how they give really amazing orgasms." Keep on bringing it up every few days

along the same lines until he finally gets it. If he never does, then your only recourse may be to haul the thing out during sex to finally gauge his reaction (see Don'ts box on p.31 for a quick recovery if he does not seem happy).

♥ Make it a game like Twenty Questions. Say, "I had a wild sex dream last night. Try to guess what happened". Once he guesses (or he may guess something you hadn't thought of which also appeals), go for it!

♥ Suggest that you both write down something new that you would like to do and then exchange notes. A simple "Whose idea should we try first?" might be all it takes.

♥ Mention that you've heard or read about some interesting techniques that sound exciting.

♥ Rent one of the *Sex and The City* episodes that features sex toy use. "The Turtle and The Hare", where Charlotte becomes addicted to her Rabbit vibrator; "Take Me Out the Ballgame", which has Samantha breaking out her vibrator with a dud stud and "Attack of the Five Foot Ten Woman" where Miranda's cleaner discovers her vibrator, are just a few classics.

♥ Show this book to your lover. You can say the girls got it for you at work as a laugh. *

♥ The next time you're renting a movie together, laugh and ask him if he wants to check out the X-

28

rated section – you can make a joke of it by saying that some of the titles are really naff and you and your mates always have a good giggle over them. Once you have him where you want him, nudge him towards renting one – look for something that has some girl on girl action as that will probably feature sex toys. And chances are, once you're watching, he'll probably nod enthusiastically if you mention that you want to try a remote control vibrator the next time you get together with his boss.

♥ Make a bet with him that he can't win and make the penalty that he has to buy a toy (suggestion: don't make it a double dildo). This gives you wiggle room to turn it into a joke if he seems at all uncomfortable.

♥ Say, "Check out what I got at that hen party I went to."

♥ Order a catalogue, slip it in with your post when he's around and act surprised that it's there ("I never ordered this!"). It's a short hop, skip and jump from there to checking out the merchandise and suggesting which ones would be fun to try.

If you're bold:

♥ The strategy is not to be so upfront that you scare him off. Begin with a question like, "Have you ever tried this?", "Do you think this would be fun?", "Do you think it would be fun to wear a costume?", "Have you ever been tied up?" or "I heard a guy's bottom is an erogenous zone – what do you think?". The vagueness of the question lets you back down if he seems inclined to start edging towards the door.

Tone is important. Keep it playful and flirtatious, so no one ends up embarrassed.

If you feel confident that he'll be up for it, you can ask the question when you're in bed (let the games begin right there and then). If you're unsure of how he'll react, introduce the topic outside of the bedroom so it can seem more theoretical and teasing. Then, if he's approachable, all it takes is a "Let's give it a try" to move the game into the mattress arena.

♥ Give him your sex toy of choice as a birthday gift (the less phallic looking, the better initially). *

♥ Guys love gadgets. They don't write in their diary, they input into their personal digital assistant. They'd never paint the house without some diesel-powered machine with a nozzle. And you know how territorial they get with the TV remote. So present using a sex toy in the same way: as a fabulous new gadget or power tool (these are all magic words to him) to use during sex.

♥ Say, "I can't wait to get you into bed.

There's something I want to show you." What he is going to hear at first is, "Bed bed bed bed bed". When "There's something I want to show you" finally filters in, he is already so hot that you could show him pictures of your great aunt Sadie naked and he would be okay with it because he has already had the promise of sex and is turned on.

♥ Ask him if he wants a threesome. Or rather, a two-and-a-halfsome. Then bring in a partner – a tiny, overexcited partner. *

♥ Challenge your lover to a no-touching orgasm. Then hand him his-and-hers remote vibrators. *

♥ Ask him, "Want to see me come in three minutes?" When he accepts your challenge (and what red-blooded male wouldn't?), hand him a prettily wrapped box containing whatever sex toy you love (beginners should try the Pocket Rocket – see Chapter 5, p.50). *

♥ *Star Wars* is a favourite fantasy with guys – hand him a baton-shaped vibrator or dildo saying, "You, Luke Skywalker; me, Princess Leia." Then watch him brandish his new light sabre.

♥ Tell him that *Rider* magazine says a ride with a vibrator is better (and considerably cheaper) than a ride on a Harley Chopper.

If you're fed up:

♥ We need sex toys. And why do we need them? BECAUSE I WANT THEM, GODDAMNIT! *

(*don't try on a brand-new lover)

STEP TWO

He is either going to go for it (hurrah) or need some convincing.

While it would be nice to think the argument that you will have a phantasmagorical orgasm and so will he should cut it, it probably won't be enough to sway him. Everyone can be a little squeamish about new things – especially when it comes to sex. This goes double when the new thing is something that hones in on what he – in his alpha way – thinks of as his territory: making you groan and moan. You're saying, "More fun" but he's hearing, "I don't need your penis". In which case, your mission is to convince him that using a sex toy will not be a replacement dick; rather, it's an add-on to try occasionally.

Be prepared to deal with just about anything, including feelings of inadequacy, emotional discomfort and ignorance (memorize "12 Things You Think About Sex Toys That Are Wrong Wrong Wrong!" from Chapter 1 to give your responses solid ground).

If you have trouble reaching orgasm, you might mention that using a vibrator would mean less work for him.

THE DON'TS

What not to do when bringing your boyfriend and sex toys together and how to jump back in case you didn't read this section before you tried to make the introduction.

DON'T bring out your vibrator for the first time in the middle of sexual play.
RECOVERY: If he jumps up screaming, "What's that noise? The bed's shaking", laugh and say, "Oh no! Somehow my back massager got into bed."

DON'T whip out a vibrator and then give it all the attention, making him feel like the third wheel.
RECOVERY: Wipe his memory banks clean by giving him an amazing blowjob – and swallowing. Next time, don't make the vibrator the focus of your play. Make sure it's tossed aside and end the play with your partner, at least for the first few times. This shows him that you are truly satisfied with him.

DON'T say, "We have to use an anal vibrator because you never touch me back there and it's the only way I am going to have an orgasm." Saying things like, "You don't do this" and "You don't do that" will send him playing for the defence.
RECOVERY: Back down by saying dreamily, "But I do love it when you do that thing with your tongue" and then give him a big smooch.

DON'T make it sound like sex is going to suck unless you bring your playmate to bed or he ties you up.
RECOVERY: Tell him that sex with him is great – better than great and occasionally adding a little fun and games into your play will just make a fantastic thing better.

DON'T bring up the subject at a bad time – like right after sex. He'll think you're not satisfied with him. Wait until you are about to have sex or, if you think he's into it, the middle of a love clinch.
RECOVERY: Yawn and say, "I don't want to talk about this right now. That orgasm you gave me totally wore me out."

DON'T give him an "It's me and my sex toy or no sex at all" ultimatum. You may end up alone, crying into your vibrator.
RECOVERY: Distract him by quickly adding, "… until you promise me that we are going to do it all night".

DON'T tell him jokes (Why did God make men? Because vibrators can't mow the lawn).
RECOVERY: Blame your boss, saying she told it to you at work and you had to faux laugh.

> No sex toy can improve a relationship, it can only enhance sex.

> *Think:*
> once you master plunging into topics like lite bondage and nipple clamps, discussing money or your mother or a flirtatious ex-girlfriend with him should be a piece of cake.

problem solvers

THE HITCH	THE FIX	SNAG	
He's a fast shooter.	Try a spray that slightly numbs him when applied to his penis.	The spray can rub off on your genitals, slowing things down for you too, so apply sparingly.	X
Your hand gets tired masturbating him.	A vibrating masturbation sleeve made of lifelike material.	The silky flesh-like material plus a variable speed vibrator will give him a sensation not even the most nimble hand job can provide.	XX
His tongue crumples during oral sex.	**Choice one:** flavoured lubricant – it will taste so good he won't want to stop. **Choice two:** bring out a vibrating tongue. It provides exquisite vibrations along with the warmth, wetness and loving licks usually received from your lover's tongue.	**Choice one:** none. **Choice two:** it may be better at licking you to orgasm than your lover is.	**Choice one:** X **Choice two:** XXX
He droops midway.	A cock ring will keep him in position beyond the call of duty.	He may want to keep on going when you're tuckered out.	XX
You have trouble reaching orgasm.	A vibrator that massages your clitoris.	You may not want to stop.	XXX
Things are dry.	Lubrication will keep things moist.	None.	XX
There's no fun in it any more.	Spice up your arsenal with some lite bondage tools like handcuffs, hot wax, blindfolds, leather or Spandex outfits.	Your trysts will require a little more planning than usual.	XXX
He's peanut-sized.	Blow him up with a penis extender – a phallic-like dildo with a soft, nubbed pocket for the penis designed to add size and girth, which is often held in place via a harness.	Might slide off during sex.	X (XXX for him – the nubs rub against him during sex).
He's on permanent wilt.* * There are many different reasons an erection may go AWOL, from depression to different medications, stress or certain illnesses. Any man who has trouble raising the flag on a regular basis should first get himself checked out by a doctor, before self-treating with a sex toy.	Penis pumps (these create suction, drawing more blood into the penis and temporarily hoisting his half-mast), combined with a cock ring to keep his flag raised during the action.	You need a good seal for the pump to work and then have to work quickly to slide the ring on before he sags again.	XX once he gets on solid ground.

5 last answers to those questions you have about using sex toys with your partner but are afraid to ask

If I suggest using a sex toy, will my boyfriend tell all his mates?
Generally, guys steer clear from the nitty-gritty's of sex revelations because they do not want images of their naked friends and their sexploits popping up mid-coitus, when they least expect it. Which is why the most they will let loose is that they slept with a woman or did not sleep with a woman. They keep it pretty brief. With two notable expectations:

Exception #1: a significant sexual shocker. He will probably tell his friends when he does or sees something truly remarkable. However, since he does not want his friends to jump to (erroneous and uneducated) guesses about his sexual prowess, he will most likely keep it to himself that you gave him a vibrating glow-in-the-dark cock ring for Valentine's Day. However, if you dig out a butt plug and demand he ram it up himself, anything goes gossip-wise.

Exception #2: a significant sexual achievement. He will tell his friends when he crosses something off The Universal Male Checklist of Studs that he wants to accomplish before he dies – such as tying you up. It's a good litmus test – if you don't trust a guy to keep it between you, him and your toy, then what were you doing playing with him anyway?

I'd like to visit a sex shop with my boyfriend, but he's too embarrassed to go. How can I convince him it'll be a laugh?
Visiting an online store first where you can shop in the privacy of your own space might not score so high for him on the blush-o-meter. Or order a catalogue and leaf through it while cosied up in bed together.

I told my boyfriend that I wanted to try a dildo and now he's convinced that I'm not satisfied with his penis size.

And they say women suffer from penis envy! Some guys are under the mistaken impression that if a flexi-penis – vibrating or otherwise – is thrown into the mix, it means they're somehow lousy lovers. Any woman with a pulse knows that these battery-powered gizmos are fun every once in a while, but there will never be a machine that can open jars, get stuff off high shelves, pay for dinner and keep you warm at night. Now you just have to convince him!

Your best bet is to forget the dildo for now and say, "Okay, I can see you're not crazy about having another penis-shaped object in bed with us, so how about a toy just for you?"

If his attitude is, "I don't need those things, I'm huge," you could say, "It's not what you have, but what you do with it that matters, and sex toys let you do a whole lot more with it." Then give him incentive by adding, "I bet you a blow job that there's no way you'll ever have the balls to use a sex toy." Be sure to come prepared so you can whip out his own –

ta dah! – vibrating cock ring. (You don't have to mention that while it's buzzing his penis and balls into orbit, your clitoris is also getting a treat.)

Once he rises to meet the challenge (one that no man could resist), he'll realize that sex toys are for his delight too and he'll probably be more willing to experiment.

He freaked out when I suggested we try_____.

Drop whatever it is you are doing and talk to him about it. The longer you wait, the harder and weirder it will be. Make sure he knows that you don't need _____ for it to be good for you (if that's the case – if not, then you need to find yourself a like-minded partner). Then give some alternatives – maybe what you suggested was just too out there. Suggest trying flavoured body paint or erotic massage oil. Then get him to help you pick it out.

This will serve two purposes: **1)** it will get you two talking easily again; and **2)** it's a gentle way to introduce him to the wide and wonderful world of sex toys

I've heard stimulating a man's prostate can be a turn-on. Are there toys just for this?

Babe, there's a toy for everything. The prostate – aka Male G-spot – is located just behind the pubic bone below the bladder, close to the root of the penis. When massaged, he sees fireworks.

There are a few things to think when choosing a toy for newbie prostate love: the toys size, flexibility, shape and, of course, safety.

Safety first – mostly because it's the easiest to deal with. Make sure you choose an anal toy with a flared safety base (usually those sold specifically for anal use) or you may lose your toy permanently.

Next, eliminate all anal dildos and vibrators that don't have a slight curve near the tip. This arc is what makes it possible for the vibrator or dildo to reach the prostate (when inserted, the curve should point forwards towards the belly button).

Now choose the smaller toys left on the table. You can always work your way up to the bigger sizes. Next, opt for those made from a softer, more flexible material such as silicone (easy to clean – important when you consider where it's making a bull's eye).

Last, stock up on plenty of lubricant. Look for those made for anal use as they tend to be thicker and sometimes even come with a slight numbing chemical to make entry easier.

BEST BOY TOYS

♥ Masturbation sleeves: for all those guys who use everything from couch cushions, toilet paper rolls and apple pie to get off.

♥ Cock rings: these could keep him going for hours, but twenty minutes should be enough to satisfy and keep his penis from being put on bed rest.

♥ Vibrating cock ring with clitoral stimulator: this takes the classic cock ring to a whole new level – one you can get off on too. Put it on right side up, and his penis and your clitoris get a buzz; flip it upside down and his balls get to play.

♥ Pouchy condoms: he'll actually be thrilled to put one on.

♥ Vibrating pumps: he can experience a buzz-and-suck combo.

♥ Vibrating vaginas, anuses and lips: enough said.

CHAPTER 3
moisturize, moisturize, moisturize!

Everyone could use a **LITTLE EXTRA JUICE** in their **sex life**. It doesn't matter if you're going to **rub it on**, **INSERT IT** or **immerse yourself** in it. It doesn't matter if you're as juicy as an overripe peach when you get going. It doesn't even matter if you're going to be playing in the water. You're going to need **LUBRICATION** (especially if you are playing in the water – it washes away all your home-produced liquids). Think must-have rather than accessory. In fact, **A TUBE OF LUBE** may be the most important sex aid in your toy box. These ointments are specifically manufactured to make your lovemaking sensual, sexy, smooth and safe (not to mention **SATISFYING**).

If you want a preview on what sex can feel like when you don't have enough moisture, wrap the forefinger and thumb of one hand around a finger of the other hand and rub up and down. Carpet burn, anyone? The same thing will happen when using sex toys – or even his penis, for that matter – without lubrication. Think about it: the easier something can slide in and out of you – whether it be the real deal or a buzzing version – the better your sexperience will be.

However, lubes are not made to just squirt and insert. Squeeze out too much or put it on too soon and you could end up with a sticky, oily mess on your hands, in your hair and just about everywhere else – not exactly the steamy scenario you had hoped for.

Here's a handy guide to all things slippery and sensual.

Choose your lube

Gone are the days when your choice was K-Y Jelly or ... K-Y Jelly. There's a type of lube available to suit every taste – literally. They come in different flavours, textures, colours and levels of stickiness.

Despite this wide array of choice, there are really only three basic types of dressing:
◆ oil-based
◆ water-based
◆ silicone-based

Oil sounds like the more slippery, slick and easy to get a hold of (just reach in the fridge for a scoop of marg) option. But oil and sex don't really mix. For one thing, oil – even if it's the kind you'd happily dip your baguette in – can make a mess of your vagina. It's hard to wash off and can throw off the vagina's normal acidic balance. This can create a haven for bacteria which in turn can lead to infections such as yeast setting up shop.

Also, oil is a bad match with latex as well as some silicone-based products. Which is why you should never, ever, ever – and I mean even in a pinch when you are just about to have the most amazing sex of your life and your lube has run out and all there is in the house is a jar of Vaseline – never use an oil or petroleum-based product with any latex or silicone sex toy or condom. The oils in these products will eat holes in the material and destroy it faster than you can say, "Oh! Oh! Oh-yesssss!"

Then there's the problem of staining – this stuff will stain the sheets, the sofa, the carpet, your French Maid's outfit, even your thong.

Silicone lubes are waterproof and last a long time. Best of all, because they never get absorbed into your skin or evaporate the way a water-based lube may, they can be reactivated with a little water or spit (take note, all you savvy shoppers: you never need more than a dab of silicone lube at a time). Of course, that pit-bull quality also means you and your toys will need a good rub with soap and water to get rid of the stuff.

Also, you should never use a silicone-based lubricant with your silicone toy. They are not well-matched because silicone is essentially made of tiny glass beads. When the beads rub together – as when you dab a blob of silicone lube on your new Vixen dildo – they scratch one another, taking that silky slick finish off of your toy.

That leaves water-based lubes. The new generation is no-muss and no-fuss: they're super-slippery, sensuous, odourless, non-sticky, non-greasy; they clean up easily and are even better at lubricating than some oil-based products. And they last ages.

As the name implies, these lubricants are made mostly of water that feels slick to the touch. The rest of the ingredients in most of these products are basically the same; what differs is their texture. Some are thicker, some thinner.

The only drawback to these lubes is that they tend to dry out after a while so you'll have to keep on reapplying if you're having a long sex session.

Now think about what you want most in a lubricant:

38

If you ...	Then use...	Why
have hypersensitive skin or are at all allergic	water-based lubricants.	They're hypoallergenic
are planning on vaginal penetration	water-based lubricants.	How much juice you produce depends on where you are in your hormonal cycle – a little extra moisture can only make things more delightfully squishy (see p.40 for more).
think you may try anal penetration	oil-based lubricants are best for a tight squeeze as long as the condom or toy are not latex-based (see above) because they're generally thicker than other types of lubricant, making entry easier (the rectum tends to absorb lubes of thinner consistencies quickly).	Look for one that has a desensitizer (think "relaxing" rather than "numbing"). Otherwise, go for a water-based lubricant specially made for bottom play. Lubrication is an absolute must for any type of anal penetration. Your anus is thin-skinned and easily torn (which is why being safe is also mandatory as this form of sexual activity is high risk for HIV infection), nor does it produce its own juices.
are going to play with his penis (or he is)	any water-based or silicone-based lube.	A little extra moisture on the penis during masturbation cuts down on the unpleasant kind of friction so he can concentrate on the sexy rub-down you're giving him.
will be using sex toys	silicone-based lubes work fine as long as your toy isn't made of the same material (see p.23). However, water-based lubes can mindlessly and safely be used on virtually any toy you have in your bag of tricks, including your silicone ones.	Unlike the penis and vagina, sex toys do not come with their own built-in lubricant. Many are manufactured from materials – particularly those made of jelly and lifelike materials – that absorb your natural lubricant, drying you out. And cock rings slide on and off much easier with extra grease.
think you may be indulging in some mouth-watering sex	go for a flavoured lube, guaranteed to tantalize your taste buds while lubricating your lover.	First, you kindle the taste buds with no bitter aftertaste. Second, who hasn't had the occasional bout of dry mouth when in the middle of giving oral action?
are planning on water play	silicone-based lubes.	Surprisingly, water play is not naturally wet sex – the water tends to wash away your own natural juices, making added lubrication a must.
simply want the best	Liquid Silk mimics your body's natural lubrication and comes in a super-handy pump bottle. Bonus: you can accidentally roll around on the bottle in the throes of passion and it doesn't squish out onto everything. Hydra-Smooth tastes better than Liquid Silk and is also good for you: it has the vitamins A, E and Aloe Vera in it.	Liquid Silk looks a lot like his love juices – although this may be a plus for you. They're both also on the high end of the price scale.

Oil slicks

It's not always obvious which products to beware of when shopping for a lube to wear with your favourite latex toy. All of the following contain oil or substances which nuke latex within an hour:

* Many body cold creams, lotions and moisturizers
* Baby powder
* Petroleum jelly
* Massage oil
* Vaginal yeast infection medication (cream or suppositories)
* Butter and/or margarine
* Any edible oil
* Rubbing alcohol
* Burn medication
* Haemorrhoidal ointments
* Sun cream
* Chocolate syrup
* Whipped cream
* Anything containing vitamin E
* Ice cream

BARGAIN BOX

As with most things in life, you get what you pay for. There's a reason some lubes cost more: they're higher in quality, you don't need to use as much and they last longer. So don't skimp your pleasure with a cheaper brand. First, check the ingredient list – generally the less-expensive lubricant will be missing out on some vital building block. Then create your own sample pack by buying a few varieties in the smallest size on offer so you don't end up splashing out a lot on a lube that disagrees with you. Once you settle on what you like, stock up on the mega size so you don't run out at a crucial juncture in the proceedings.

Just add juice

Except for with anal sex, using lubricant requires a Zen attitude: less is more. Your toy should be slick, but not dripping, or you'll lose all the friction. You can always add more if you need it. The general rule of thumb is that if it doesn't slide in comfortably, you probably need more.

Squeeze/pour a small amount onto your palm. Then spread it wherever the party is going to take place – on yourself, your partner and/or any part of your toy that is going to come in contact with you.

Keep the dressing light – it should be glossy but not drenched. Keep your touch light when rubbing or you will end up moisturizing your hand instead of your toy or essential bits.

If you're using a toy with a harness, use a water-based lubricant if the toy does not fit easily through the opening.

Circumcised men tend to be a bit stiff around the collar – a dab of lubricant helps unbend them and make them putty in your hands.

moisturize, moisturize!

5 last answers to those questions you have about lubing-up but are afraid to ask

Do I have to use a commercial lubricant or can I use anything lying around the house?

Since you're planning on rubbing this stuff on a part of your body that you hold near and dear – your genitals – it's best to use something designed by many of the brightest and best minds specifically for that purpose. However, in a pinch, you can use a water-based body lotion (especially if it's marked "hypoallergenic").

What's the best his-and-hers lube?

Astroglide. Originally created by NASA scientists (and you thought I was joking about the brightest and best minds), it's unscented, sweet-tasting, latex-safe and slippery enough to make your lower regions smile for hours.

I get pretty wet on my own – do I really need extra lubrication?

Absolutely. For one thing, droughts happen – particularly at the end of your cycle. Also, you are going to dry up if you have a marathon lovemaking session. And if you are planning to include sex toys in your play, chances are that the outer shell will absorb your natural lubrication, turning your vagina into a desert. Lastly, extra juice actually acts as a stimulant, intensifying sensation. On the other hand, too little wetness can lead to painful sex, sore/burning genitals for days after, a bladder infection or vaginal infections. Convinced?

Should I look for a lube that has nonoxynol-9?

You decide: nonoxynol-9 is basically a type of detergent commonly used in everything from baby wipes to contraceptive foams. While it has been shown to be moderately successful at killing sperm, it can also put the user more at risk of being infected with HIV when used with an infected partner by as much as fifty per cent. On a less hazardous note, it can also be irritating to sensitive skin.

What's wrong with using saliva as a lube?

You can – but expect to keep on spitting since saliva evaporates after a few seconds (somehow, I don't think turning your lover into a spittoon is exactly the sexy moment you were going for). So splash out on some lube.

If you're greasing up yourself or your lover, warm up the lubricant first by pouring it into your hands and then rubbing them together.

CHAPTER 4
taking care of business

If you learned one thing from your MOTHER, it's this: take **CARE** of your toys. Sure, it seems a whole lot easier just to throw your VIBRATORS and DILDOS into the TOP DRAWER and forget about them until the next time. But keeping your sex toy **CLEAN** and happy will help to prolong its life and help to keep you healthy. Almost any kind of sex toy can – and will – come in contact with **bodily fluids** of one kind or another. And when it comes to sexually transmitted infections, a DIRTY PIECE of penis-shaped rubber can be just as toxic as its real flesh-and-blood counterpart. So you need to properly remove these fluids. Plus if you're planning on sharing your toys with a friend, it's just good manners to keep things on the **SPIC-AND-SPAN** side.

Cleaning up

A step-by-step guide (those with a more laid-back approach to life can read step one and then skip ahead to the last step).

1 Usually a thorough wash with soap (the anti-bacterial kind is best) and hot water after use is enough to make your toy sparkle and infection-free (the only exception to this rule is with lifelike materials like Futurotic® and Cyberskin™ products – see Step 3). But rinse well – soapy dregs can cause damage to the toy (not to mention irritate your tender bits and pieces). If your toy is battery-operated or electric, do not submerge it in water unless it is specifically marked that it is water-proof. Otherwise you may burn the motor and corrode the battery compartment, causing it to short out. Ouch!

You can also clean and disinfect with a commercial cleanser specifically made for sex toys like Safe Suds (available from any adult shop – see Resources). You spray it on the toy, let it sit a couple of minutes and wipe away. These cleansers are great for battery operated toys that can't be put under water to clean.

2 If your sex toy is made of*:
• Silicone: this super-hero tough material is non-porous and hypoallergenic which makes it a cinch to clean. You can throw it in the top rack of the dishwasher (although perhaps not when the dishes are there), boil it for a few minutes (as long as it has no plastic add-ons which can become damaged in ultra hot water) or just use the soap and water method described in Step 1.

• Lifelike materials: this stuff is a lot like skin (it even wrinkles when touched!), which means it needs a little extra TLC to keep it looking (and working) at its best. It also means the surface is very porous – translation: ideal breeding ground for nasty infections. All of which means that you need to use just warm water and then rub, gently, with a cloth dampened with rubbing alcohol (but make sure you rinse it thoroughly unless pain is part of your sexual repertoire). There is also a special solution just for Cyberskin™ (most Cyberskin™ toys come with a sample kit to get you started).

• Latex/rubber: the cheap and chic of the sex toy set, toys made out of latex

43

*see Chapter 1, pp.22-25 for advice on choosing materials

are fairly durable and don't need special care beyond the soap and swab method described in Step 1.

• Jelly: a less-pricey alternative to silicone, jelly toys are also very porous – which means your best bet for staying infection-free is to use some of those savings to invest in a special sex toy cleaner (see Resources). Never clean your jelly toys with rubbing alcohol as it will melt your toy into a rubbery mess.

• Plastic, Acrylic, Metal or Glass: easy-peasy – water and a washcloth or swab it with rubbing alcohol (remembering to rinse it afterward.

3 ATTENTION! LAST STEP!: If all the above seems like too much hassle, then slipping a condom over your vibrator, dildo or anal plug during use will make clean-up a snap. Simply peel it off and throw it away.

Never double dip – if you used your toy vaginally, then slip a condom over it or give it a good scrub down (see Cleaning Up, p.43) before entering via the back door (and vice versa).

No matter how much you love your sex gadget, do not pamper it by drying it in fluffy towels after giving it a sponge down. The fluff will leave lint which can act like low-grade sandpaper on your privates. Also, your sex toy could grab any bacteria in the towel. Use a lint-free towel or let the toy air-dry.

44

House rules for putting your toys away

♥ Make sure you keep your toy in a place where it won't collect a lot of dust or animal hair. Every tiny particle in the air will stick to some materials, especially jelly rubber. Wrapping it in a clean, lint-free hanky or an old clean T-shirt is a low-maintenance way to protect the surface.

♥ Also store your toys in a cool dry place (in other words, not the bathroom or a damp cellar). Constant exposure to moisture can cause the material on many sex toys to decay or disintegrate.

♥ Don't jumble your toys into one big pile when you store them – when sex toys are left to rub up against each other for long periods of time, the latex will begin to disintegrate and the jellies will melt into one another.

♥ If your toy has batteries, take them out when you're not using it. This will not only keep the batteries from leaking and ruining your toy, it's also a thrifty move for prolonging the life of your battery.

♥ Don't put your toy where your dog or cat might find it and mistake it for a fab new prezzie from the pet shop.

DON'T EVEN THINK ABOUT SKIPPING THIS NEXT BIT

It can't be said too often: YOU CAN GET AN STI FROM USING A SEX TOY.

So, just a few general facts on STIs (sexually transmitted infections) that you may not know, once knew and forgot or need to read again and again because – let's face it –they may save your life:

♥ Condoms can't protect you from everything.

♥ Some STIs (such as HIV, herpes and genital warts) are for life – there is no cure, only medication to control them.

♥ Most STIs have no symptoms – that's zilch, zero, nada, nothing!

♥ However, even without symptoms, many can lead to infertility and sometimes death if left untreated.

♥ You can't tell by looking if he is infected (unfair reality: he is more likely to give you an STI if he has one than you are likely to give him one if you have one).

♥ Getting an STI means your chances of getting HIV are increased.

♥ You can have more than one STI at a time and like squabbling siblings, they can make each other worse.

5 last answers to those questions you have about cleaning your sex toys but are afraid to ask

Will washing my toy really keep me safe from STIs? Probably – if you wash it well (in other words, read the steps!). Making sure your toy is thoroughly dry before putting it away will also prevent moulds and bacterial colonies from setting up camp on its surface. Using a condom if the toy is going to slip into any of your or your lover's openings also boosts your safety factor. Also be sure to change the condom if you are going to be orifice-jumping (mouth to vagina to bottom and so on). Think of it this way: sharing a sex toy with a partner is the same as having sex with that partner. So take all the same precautions.

I love my vibrator, but lately I've been experiencing a slight burning sensation after using it. Chances are you didn't rinse well when cleaning it. Soap builds up after a time, causing skin reactions. Switching to a commercially-made cleaner will keep it squeaky clean so that the only fire you light is a pleasurable one.

Oops – I was washing my battery-operated vibrator and got the batteries wet. Not to worry – remove the batteries right away and blow-dry the inside of your toy's battery chamber completely.

I have a harness that is starting to reek. Can I clean it? Absolutely. To keep leather items dirt-free, soft and flexible, buy some leather conditioner (often found in tack/horse supply stores). Also, keep your leather toys away from direct heat as it will dry out the material and cause it to crack.

My vibrator seems to be made of silicone and something else. Should I just follow the instructions for cleaning a silicone toy? Silicone is often joined with other stuff – often plastic or jelly, sometimes a lifelike skin material called Neoskin®. The payoff is a hybrid toy that combines the best of all material worlds. The downside is that you can't give your toy quite the same casual abuse you could if it were 100 per cent silicone. Your best bet is to use warm water and soap or a commercial toy cleaner. Then let it air-dry completely before putting it away.

two

*vibrators
& dildos
& orgasms,
oh my!*

First, the basics:

VIBRATORS – as the name suggests – vibrate. Some can be inserted, but generally, they're made for buzzing your love button.

DILDOS, on the other hand, generally refer to a tube-shaped gizmo that is mainly designed for penetration.

Beyond that, anything goes.

The lovely reality is that these babies have changed a lot since your mother's day (get over it – sex toys have been around for centuries, so they were definitely around when your parents were busy sexperimenting). Pity the poor women in the seventies who used the standard 18cm (7 inch), penis-like rubber toy that dominated the scene for years. These archaic vibrators were loud, bulky, short-lived and one speed. If a woman wanted to take her vibrations on the road, she needed a separate suitcase just for her toy!

Thanks to advances in technology, today's woman can actually buzz off in public either on her own or with the help of her partner without anyone being any the wiser. Best of all, as manufacturers learn more about this technology, the range of the remotes gets longer, so you and your sex toy can play further apart. Closer to home, there are vibrators so small they can fit on the tip of your finger (perfect for creating a custom-designed orgasm), collared vibrators to match your outfit du jour, vibrators so quiet even your partner won't suspect why you have a goofy grin on your face and multi-purpose buzz tools that whip, pulse and puree you into a joyful heap.

High-tech also comes to the aid of the dildo. Once made out of cold, hard, difficult-to-clean plastic, these joy sticks are now available in materials that feel just like the real thing but – unlike their flesh-and-blood counterparts – can be tossed in a pot of boiling water to get them clean afterward.

Nor do vibrators and dildos have to look like they just stumbled off of a porn set any longer. They come in a rainbow of colours and are available in just about every shape, ranging from ergonomically correct models and multi-purpose little numbers that look like this season's latest accessory to children's toys lookalikes.

You've come a long way, baby.

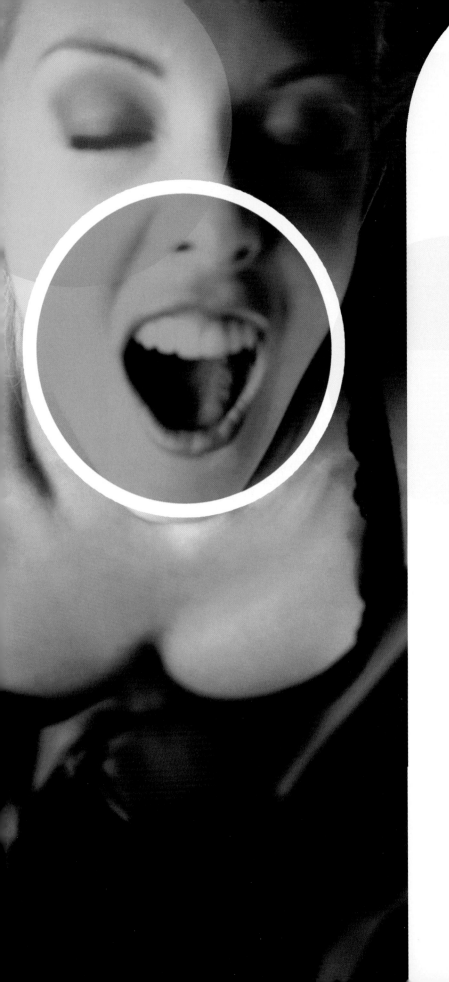

CHAPTER 5
scream machines

If you're
suddenly going blank
on how you like it, have
a quick DIY session and
check out where your
hand goes.

Everyone knows women can have more than one kind of orgasm: There's the "Ooh, ooh, mmm, that's nice, mmmm" orgasm, there's the "Ohmigod, YESYESYES, I'M COMINGGGGGGG" orgasm – and then there's everything in between.

Since supply and demand go hand in hand, there are vibrators for every kind of cha cha cha. The hard part is figuring out what you want. Unfortunately, vibrators don't come with need-specific info. In fact, despite having evolved way beyond the switch it on and turn on stage, they barely come with user-friendly instructions at all. Before you go ga-ga eyed looking at what's available out there, read this list to get the general gist of what it is you want your new power tool to do for you. You're not on a pleasure budget, so check off as many points as you like. Note that some vibrators are multifunctional:

Are you an innie or an outie?

As amazing as vibrators today are, yours won't magically know what you like most when you use it (in that way, they're really no better than your average male). So think where you want the action: on your clitoris (outie), in your vagina (innie) or – you greedy guts – every which way (innie/outie) and purchase appropriately.

Innies are specifically made to work like a penis and be thrust into the vagina with the added ooh-la-la of vibrating, rotating or giving some other kind of internal buzz. While they miss out on your love button entirely, many have curved tips or knobbed sides to give your G-spot a friendly nudge (see G-spot point, p.52).

Innie shortlist: Anything from the Slim line, Magnumbullet (one of the few bullets designed extra long for insertion), Micro Pleasure Egg, Pink Pearl.

Outies give you love where you most need it: right on your clitoris (while most vibrators can be used around the clitoris, their vibrations may be too strong for your bundle of joy to take). Usually small and compact (making them great for travel), they don't have fancy shafts topped with gizmos or gadgets. What they do have are heads, balls, bullets or eggs designed to stimulate the clitoris (many are controlled by a small remote attached to a thin wire). Few look like what they really are. Some are even shaped like cats, bunnies, bears, dewdrops, miniature rocket vibrators and large human tongues. Whichever design you choose, basic operation is the same – focused vibrations at varying speeds and intensities.

If you're using an innie bullet, pull it out with your fingers instead of pulling on the cord to avoid embarrassing accidents.

49

Outie shortlist: Jelly Cliterrific, Remote Clit Blaster, Dancing Dolphin, I-Vibe Pocket Rocket, Micro Pleasure Egg, Pocket Rocket, Fukuoku 9000, Micro Butterfly, Private Pocket Rocket, Mini Pearl, Double Bullets, Cyber Flicker, Ultra 7 Bullet.

Innie/outies, aka dual-action vibrators, are the best of both worlds. Be warned: they do require a little finesse to master so they're probably not for beginners. However, once you do get it down, these lovelies are a fairly hassle-free way to go over the edge. Usually a dual-action vibrator has a rotating or vibrating dildo for vaginal penetration, along with a clitoral stimulator. The two parts move independently, and each has its own control, so they can be adjusted to mood. The clitoral attachment is usually shaped like an animal – mainly because the Japanese came up with the idea and in Japan, anatomically-correct sex toys are a no-no. Skip the cute arm imagery and think of this tool as an extra hand.

Innie/outie shortlist: I-Vibe Rabbit, Jack Rabbit, Panther, Pearl Butterfly, Rabbit Pearl, Lollipopper, Supreme Indulgence, The Translucent Butterfly, The Deep Penetrating Latex Dong.

The free batteries that come with the vibrator are often cheap and weak, so splurge and get some Alkaline batteries before powering up.

Skip the dual action if thrusting is essential for your orgasm - that's one thing they can't provide.

Contrary to myth, mains-powered vibrators won't blow up or burn you, although some manufacturers suggest that you turn them off for a rest after a half hour, especially if you're burning rubber at high speed.

Rechargeable vibrators are versions of the wand that have built-in, rechargeable nickel-cadmium batteries. You plug them in to charge up, then detach the cord to allow for about half an hour of unencumbered, swinging-from-the-chandeliers fun.

50

What kind of power play are you into?

The two major categories for vibrators are mains-powered and battery-operated. Check out their positives and negatives and decide what kind of charge you want:

	+ CHARGE	- CHARGE	SHORTLIST
MAINS-POWERED	A powerhouse, they're very good at what they do, quieter than most, provide intense vibrations, and are reliable – they won't conk out at the moment of truth. They're strong enough to massage other parts of your body such as your neck or back, easily available at your corner chemist and not particularly hard on the electric bill. They have extra attachments (like a Swiss Army knife) to make them good to go for penetration.	Limited range of motion and limited usage in that they're a little too strong for using like a penis. They're expensive, with the visual charm of a hand blender. The attachments can be fiddly, big and ugly. Not for the timid.	Hitachi Magic Wand, E Vibe Body Massager, Wahl 7-in-1, Wahl 2-Speed All Body Massager.
BATTERY	More convenient as you don't have to have a where's-the-power-point search. There's a jaw-dropping selection, they're cheap and portable – some are even waterproof. You can select one to hit just your G-spot or whatever spot you choose.	Like a bad ex, they have no staying power – you need to plan ahead and keep batteries in stock (unless you go for a rechargeable – see Tipbit opposite). Some of the cheaper ones are poor quality and cheesy looking. The plastic cracks easily if you drop it when you experience Big Bang.	Silver Bullet, Honey Bear, Amethyst Shimmer, Cascading Climaxer, I-Vibe Pocket Rocket, I-Vibe Rabbit, Jack Rabbit, Little Bunny, Mach X20 Probe, Micro Pleasure Egg, Oasis Pleasure Probe, Pearl Butterfly, Pocket Rocket, Rabbit Pearl, White Orchid.

You still have the same clunky, big mobile phone you originally got several years ago.

Then you want your basic traditional vibrator. When people think of vibrators, this is usually the style that comes to mind. Vaguely resembling a penis, they lack the bells and whistles of your more fancy jobs. The most complicated option is a multi-speed switch that lets you control the power of your buzz so using them seems more like traditional intercourse, with a big, pulsating bonus. They also nicely fit the measurements of your true-to-life penis, stretching from 10–20cm (4–8 inches). It's always best to start small and work your way up.

SHORTLIST: Jelly Flex Clitterific, Latex Stud, Flexi-vibe, Pink Dot Vibe, Temptress Tiger, Violet Fantasy, White Orchid, Dome Tip Satisfier, Hide-a-Vibe, Racquel Slimline, Tropical Vibrations, Pulse-Right Bullet Vibe (this last one is the original model that all other pulsatrons were based on).

Traditional vibrators are simple and easy, making them ideal for vibe virgins.

Break out with an I-surge vibe — it's not hard to work the controls and it comes in a range of candy colours.

Remember, you don't have to be monogamous with your sex toys. The more you have, the more different types of fun you'll have.

I want to finally find out where the hell my G-spot is.

Your G-spot is a hotspot located on the upper wall of your vagina. When pressed, it can make you gush orgasm after orgasm. But you need to hit it directly to get the pleasure pay-off – not an easy task when you're working blind, so to speak. Trying to ring its bell with fingers can be very hit and miss. With a G-spot vibrator, you'll be finding it again … and again … and again. Usually slender with a slight curve at the end, they look a lot like a crooked finger. Some have a textured base to caress your outie love button at the same time.

SHORTLIST: Insatiable G, Marina Opulent Slender G, Chasey Lain Slimline G, G Spot Fantasy Massager, G Spot Multi Speed Vibe, Virtual Skin G-spot Massager, Nubby G, Clearly G.

Do you want to share the love?

While you and your lover can use almost any vibrator together, pure vibration isn't usually as appealing to men as it is to women. However, some toys combine suction, subtle pressure and other forms of male-friendly impulses while finger vibes are gentle enough to happily melt his penis in your hands. Remember too that some men are more secure than others and are not going to shrink (everywhere) at the sight of a 18cm (7 inch) faux penis while others will start comparing it to themselves – centimetre by centimetre (see Boy Toys, p.94).

SHORTLIST: Impulse i5 Opulence, the Pulsatron series, which has every accessory under the sun for his and her vibrating pleasure (see Sexessorize!, p.59), Fukuoku Power Pack, Micro Finger Tickler.

Did you just inherit some money?

Vibrators range from a few pounds to a few hundred (yes, you read correctly – apparently, pure pleasure isn't free). The more you shell out, the more whirring/buzzing/spinning/rotating/fluttering extras you are going to get. However, more money does not necessarily mean more hubba hubba. Your basic one-battery operated metal or plastic shell is going to give you enough bang for your bucks. But what it won't do is give you lots of bangs over time. So if you are looking for a long-term investment, you'll need to pay up. Also, the nicer-feeling the material the vibrator is made from, the more it will cost (see Chapter 1, pp.22–5 for more on different materials). However, if you are just dipping your toes in the sex toys pool, start inexpensive and work your way up.

SAVER SHORTLIST: Silver Bullet, Celestial G, Cosmic Invader, Dazzle, Dolphin Erection Arouser, Amethyst Shimmer, Cascading Climaxer, Crystal Clear Power Vibe.

SPLURGE SHORTLIST: Cyberskin Pleasure Shell, Decadent Indulgence.

You're a club girl at heart.

Some of the newer vibes are outfitted with a device that surges with increases

Some sound-sensitive vibes also work with the voice – if you wear one out of doors, beware of anyone with a megaphone.

in sound. So if you're listening to music, they'll correspond to the beat. The louder the music, the stronger the vibe. You can also hook up your CD or MP3 player directly to the controller so your music or audio tracks are directly translated into custom pulses for your own private, orgasmic dance party.

SHORTLIST: Audi-Oh.

I don't want a toy penis lying around the house.

Then avoid the stress and still pleasure yourself – go for a model that looks like anything but what it is. One option is any of Candice Royalle's natural contoured vibrators. These body-sculpted massagers have a slight hourglass shape ergonomically designed to fit the female body. (For vibrators discreet enough to pass any security check, see Spot the Vibe, p.54.)

SHORTLIST: Magnifique, Jolie, Petite, Superbe, Ultime.

The mains-powered vibes are the longest-living vibes on the market (some Hitachi Magic Wands have lasted over 20 years).

Remember that you can't please all the people all the time. What works for you might not work for your partner, so if you're expecting the toy to deliver mind-blowing simultaneous mutual orgasms, there's a good chance you'll be disappointed.

Spot the vibe

Can you spot which of the following is not a vibrator?

Answer

4. An Egg: you can scramble, poach, fry or boil it – but vibrate it and it will crack.

1 At just four inches tall, it's the same shape and size as a tube of lipstick and even has a removable cap. Just don't apply in public.

2 This vibe will be just ducky in any bathroom setting, providing quiet vibrating stimulation even in the bath or shower.

3 This pillow won't put you to sleep – it has an almost totally silent 20cm (8 inch) multi-speed vibrator.

5 It could pass for anything: an address book, a mobile phone case, a glasses case – anything except an extremely strong vibrating multi-purpose bullet vibrator.

6 This remote-controlled vibrating egg is so discreet you can actually use in public without anybody knowing.

7 Pencil thin and 11cm (4.3 inches) in length, it's a miniature sex machine!

1

2

3

4

5

6

7

If you've never done the orgasm shimmy, get a wand massager. Their powerful, insistent vibration is as close to a guarantee as the sex toy world can offer.

54

I love to dress up.

Go for a vibrator with tons of features like dual clitoral and internal stimulation and lots of different power levels and types of vibrations.

SHORTLIST: the Pulsar range comes with loads of add-on accessories (see Sexessorize!, p.59), 5X Giga Power Sex Probe, Mach X 20 Probe, Thruster Probe, Jack Rabbit Vibrators.

I don't know how to set the time on my VCR.

You want something straightforward with a simple "on/off" switch so you don't have to think beyond, "turn it on/turn it off". However, if you want more variation than a basic buzz, you'll need to overcome your technophobia.

SHORTLIST: any of the rocket series, Chasey Lain Slimline G.

Do you have to work it to supernova?

While using a vibrator definitely ups your chances of having an orgasm (and not just any old orgasm – a fabulous, brilliant, seeing stars kind of orgasm), you are going to want a bit more guarantee if you are the type of girl who always comes late to the party. While the steady vibration of your basic vibe feels great, you are going to need to customize your buzz. Look for vibrators that pulse at different speeds so you can switch back and forth from a short and steady beat to longer, more intense ones mid-play. Rotating bead vibrators that throb and ricochet off one another will also do the job, as will fingertip vibes that have a removable

stimulation pad which attaches to your finger so you can deliver the kick exactly where you need it.

SHORTLIST: Fukuoku Power Pack, Micro Finger Tickler, Angel's Touch, 5X Giga Power Sex Probe, Mach X 20 Probe, Thruster Probe, Waterproof Pleasure Pal, Mini Flex Massager.

Does size matter? (Don't tell him if the answer is yes).

For all you size queens who want a tool the size he can only fantasize about having, there is a vibrator for you. Look for anything that has words describing magnitude in the name, such as "colossal" or "titan". Just make sure you pay attention to the dimensions of these toys, as some of these giants can be the size of small pets!

BIG SHORTLIST:: Extra Thick Vibrating Cock, Thundercloud, Kong, Real Feel Vibrator.

Good things also come in small packages. Small means it is portable, fantastic for clitoral stimulation, a less intimidating plaything for him and something that can be worn under clothing.

SMALL SHORTLIST: iVibes, Mini Massager, Pocket Rocket, Waterproof Pleasure Pal, Mighty Mite, Mini Flex Massager.

If you are not sure how much thickness you want, go smaller rather than larger so you'll know your new toy will fit.

I want it as close to the real deal as possible.

If it's texture you're looking for, then these materials feel like real skin without the razor burn: Futurotic, Cyberskin™, Soft Touch or Silicone (see Material Girl, p.23). Some vibrators are like faux willies, complete with veins and head and even realistic skin colours. The only difference is that they don't conk out until you turn them off.

SHORTLIST: Cyberskin™ Vibrating Cybercock, Soft-Touch Vibrating Dong, Real Feel Vibrator, 7-Inch Ultra Realistic, Emperor 8" Vibrating Dildo, Cyber Cock.

Do you want to make your neighbours jealous?

While no vibrator is going to be perfectly silent, some are noisier than others. The rule of thumb is: the more powerful the vibrator, the louder it is. Vibrators that use C-size batteries are louder than their smaller battery counterparts, but give more intense vibrations. Vibrators made from jelly vinyl are quieter than plastic ones. Hard plastic battery vibrators like the Classic and some large wand vibrators such as Hitachi are the loudest, while coil-operated ones seem to make the least racket. Remote control products will be as quiet as a vibrating product can be.

Any vibrator can turn loud the longer it runs, the more it's used or for simply no reason at all.

Five ways to turn down the volume:

1. Turning on the stereo will mask most noise (make sure it's something that sets the mood and not this year's European Cup song).
2. Mute the noise on outie buzz sessions by placing a towel or blanket over the part of the toy that encases the engine.
3. Operate your vibrator on low power only. It won't give you as strong of a vibration, but it will be quieter.
4. Keep your vibrator under your covers with you. You'll be warm and the sound will be muffled.
5. Cover your vibrator with a jelly sleeve (see Sexessorize!, p.59). You'll lessen the noise (though the nubs on the sleeve may cause you to shout more).

However, even those listed as "whisper quiet" will make some noise since they are electrically powered. Your next-door neighbour may not hear you hitting the buzzer, but somebody outside your closed bedroom door might think you are spending a lot of time shaving your legs with the electric razor.

SHORTLIST: Tender Touch, Wahl 7-in-1, Honey Bear

How wet do you like it?

If you love playing hunt the ducky in the bath then waterproof vibrators were made for you. They can be used in the tub, shower, hot tub, ocean or anywhere you want to float your boat. They are all battery vibes with an extra seal where the batteries go and waterproof casing all around.

SHORTLIST: Octo-Pussy, Waterproof Rabbit, Jelly Clitterific, The Hawaiian Vibe.

Are you a bottoms-up girl?

If you're not opposed to coming in the back door, make sure the vibrator is made for the job. It needs to have a flared base or be attached to a retrieval cord so it doesn't slip all the way in (forcing you to make that long embarrassing trip to A&E). These vibrators can have variable speeds, internal or external power supplies, and fancy features – just like other vibrators. But be warned: anal vibrators are not pretty. They look like weird sea creatures – oblong, knobbly, spiny and bendable (see Chapter 10 for more on plug-play).

SHORTLIST: JurASSic Jewel Vibrator, Cascading Climaxer, Kiwi Gumdrop.

Do you want to multi-task a workout with your sex sesh?

Then put all your eggs in one basket with an egg vibe (think small egg). These can be used as vaginal exercise aids to help women pump up their vaginal muscles. If you are a Kegel Master (you can contract and release your vaginal muscles at will), then these are the next step up. You stay buff by inserting an egg into your vagina and holding it there – some women even add weights eventually.

SHORTLIST: Micro Pleasure Egg, The Hot Shot.

Do you want to keep your hands free for other activities?

The design of hands-free clitoral stimulators is as removed from phallic as you can get – think something that looks like a mate of Bambi. But don't be fooled by the critter's cute appearance – these mini vibrators are held snug against your clitoris for incredibly strong, intense, controlled beat. And since they can be worn out of the house, this may be just the thing to get you through the grind at work.

SHORTLIST: Pearl Butterfly, Venus Butterfly, Micro Butterfly

Do you want to go "Oh!" on the go?

Thanks to improvements in wireless technology, you can put your orgasmic destiny in your partner's hands – across a crowded room. Small, remotely-controlled egg-shaped or cylindrical vibrators are built into underwear. Discreet switches (à la garage door remote control) mean he can make you hit the ceiling from as much as 27 metres (90 feet) away.

SHORTLIST: Remote Control Butterfly, Wireless Remote Control Egg, Remote Control Torpedo, Remote Control Bear, Oyster Remote Control Vibrator, Remote Tiger Thong.

Remote control vibrators are quiet, but they are vibrators. Stick to places with a light cover of sound, and only use remote-control toys at events from which you can easily escape - nothing is worse than getting worked into a frenzy and being caught in the middle of something where you can't get out without causing a scene.

Do you want a Volvo or a Fiat?

Most vibrators are really designed as "novelties" – in other words, they might live from days to just a few short months. Mains-powered vibrators and brand-name battery vibrators last the longest if you're looking for a long-term commitment.

SHORTLIST: Hitachi, Panasonic

Do you want it all?

Why settle? Get a vibrator kit. Basic ones usually include several types of mix-and-match vibrators, a few sleeves of various shapes and sizes, and often some lubricant, maybe even feathers, blindfolds, masks, beads … you name it. Bonus: you save money when you combination buy.

SHORTLIST: Cherry Blossom, Exotic Vacation Travel Kit, G-Spot Pleasure Collection, Tropical Sensations Kit.

If he wants to play with you later, he should stay on a buzz diet with the remote control — too much pressure on your joy stick and you may barely be able to get up and leave. Make sure he knows there's a time delay between turning the remote on or off, and when the vibration actually stops or starts or there'll be times when he thinks he's put you on the down-low but you're still buzzing.

LITTLE HOUSE OF HORRORS

Some vibrators look like they were designed by the Marquis de Sade (father of painful sex). Some of these numbers look like they'll make you moan all right – in discomfort!

★ Purple Power Prickly: the spiky head looks like something from the Middle Ages – ouch!

★ Disco Light Up Vibrator: An 18cm (7 inch) vibe that lights up and changes colour when you turn it on. All it's missing is the disco ball.

★ Jelly Colossal: 3.8 cm (1½ inches) in diameter – how big can that be? Bigger than the average male penis! These are elephantine proportions! Now imagine slipping that in for a little fun.

★ Beyond 2000: Is it a plane? Is it a rocket ship? No, it's an 18cm (7 inch) pink-shafted vibrator with sparkling silver bands, glittering pearl-sized heads, contours, ridges and a charging rhino. With the silver beads spinning one way, contoured pinkness headed the other way, and a rhino charging up the middle, you end up feeling like an unbalanced wash load. Now that's sexy!

★ Vibro Explorer: the glowing end makes you feel like it's a missile launcher and you are the target. Imagine waking up and seeing it winking at you in the dark. Great if you have a habit of losing things once the lights are out.

★ Orgasmatron Vibrating Strap On: a multi-speed strap-on vibrator that actually squirts! Sort of like sleeping with a clam.

★ Bendables 8¼ inch (20cm) Vertebrae Vibe: the three metal studs may be designed to caress the clitoris, but they end up looking like a bad punk job.

★ Coil Massagers: yes, they get the job done but the design has not changed they were first marketed in the 1940s. When you use it, it makes you come over all middle-aged.

★ Technoflex: at over 25cm (10 inches) long, you will need to make sure that you have a cupboard or drawer that it will fit in, let alone a vagina that will accommodate it!

★ The Stinger: it looks like a scorpion – sexy for bug lovers, maybe.

★ Audi-Oh: Using this bullet-style vibrator is like playing funky sound with a karaoke machine. It takes what you are listening to and vibrates along with the sound. You can also input sound from audio devices like CD or MP3 players directly into it.

★ Robo Dick: This is one pound of cold, hard steel. If that doesn't do it for you, try a battering ram.

Sexessorize!

It's not what you wear – it's how you dress it up. Here are the latest fashions to accessorize your vibrator:

♥ Rings: a flexible ring allows some hands-free clitoral stimulators to be attached to a penis, dildo or hand for some love-button action during the in-and-out.

♥ Jewellery set: wand and coil-style vibes can be kitted out with everything from suction cups, butt plugs and G-spot wands to dual penetrators, cups, bulbs and soft rubber rings. Just remember: less is more.

♥ Sleeves: an inexpensive way to turn your cheap vibe into a chic vibe is to take a basic slimline vibe and spice it up with vibrator sleeves. They're made of jelly, Cyberskin™, plastic, technoskin, silicone and latex with nubs, prickles, anal attachments, mini penises and the full meat-and-two veg set of penis and balls.

♥ Belt: harnesses help keep your vibrator up (see p.73 for more on how to harness up).

♥ Lotions: Lubrication is a necessity more than it is an accessory. See Chapter 3 for the low-down.

♥ Rolls Royce: The Pulsatron series has a drawer full of accessories that cover every e-zone on your body from the Clit Seducer to the Analiscious (the names are self-explanatory).

Good Vibrations

RATING
* : It might put a smile on your face under the right circumstances
** : It'll roll your socks off
*** : Get ready to wake the neighbours

	IDENTIFYING CHARACTERISTICS	BUZZ OFF	PULL	SNAGS	FRILLS	GOOD FOR VIBRATOR VIRGINS
Eroscillator	Electric, waterproof, comes with four accessories for the vagina, clitoris, nipples and penis	**	Dr Ruth endorsed it; very quiet so he can hear your every moan.	Dr Ruth endorsed it; attachments can be fiddly.	A toy chest workhorse.	YES
Vibrating Knickers	Built-in vibrating unit, battery-operated, for remote fun.	**	You can vibrate wherever you are; a fashion accessory: they make doing the chores a snap; think – a remote you'll never lose!	Says one size fits all but it's really best for sizes 10-16; vibrations can be subtle.	Come in thong or Brazilian cut, black or white; so they go with whatever you're wearing.	YES
Hello Kitty	Made of hard bubblegum pink plastic and topped with a friendly Hello Kitty for outie vibrating.	*	Cool street stats; smooth sides make it easy to grip.	One speed: very loud purr; head a bit cumbersome; smooth sides mean little friction.	So cute you could display it on your night stand.	NO
Multi Pocket Rocket	Nubby tip for a textured feel, more functions than a food processor; waterproof and plastic.	***	The size of your middle finger (looks like a spark plug). Don't be fooled by the size – it packs more power than Schwarzenegger!	It's loud enough for a flatmate to notice and it's no good for innie use unless you slip on an attachment.	Men like it too.	YES
Wild Wiggler	Soft, jelly, flexible, multi-speed with two different wands, waterproof and battery-operated.	***	Designed on a computer for top orgasmic payoff; small; lightweight; very quiet.	Jelly unit slips off the base unit in the bath.	Friendly and discreet.	YES
Bedside Bullet	Ten mouth-watering functions for you and him.	****+	Great looking and the size of an electric toothbrush, it will get an orgasm out of a stone.	You might love it too much and run off and marry it.	Settings are progressive so you can work up to a powerful orgasm – all for less than you'd spend on dinner out.	YES
Rabbit Pearl	Soft jelly, multi-speed, two power controls: one for the vibrating, gyrating and rotating shaft with pearls, and another for the bunny-shaped clitoral teaser on the top of the Rabbit Pearl's shaft.	***	Five tools in one (adding up to 120 ways to pleasure yourself) – it's a dildo, an innie vibrator, it has a twirling shaft, revolving pearls and the rabbit head is a clitoral love bunny. It has a corded power pack making it easy to change speeds mid-play.	You need a degree in electrical engineering to figure out the controls, the top of the shaft doesn't actually vibrate so it's not great for intense clitoral stimulation.	This toy is cute enough to share.	NO

Product	Description	Rating	Pros	Cons	Verdict	Couple-friendly
	...pouch that holds a two-inch vibrator.		...keeps your hands free to wander at will during love time.	...you first dates as it takes some acrobatics to get on.	it's couple friendly, giving everyone a bit of a buzz.	YES (though the strap-on might make you feel a bit butch at first).
Magnifique	Three speeds, easy to use controls, soft, comfortable plastic and battery operated.	***	Designed by a woman with just one thing in mind – you. An innie and an outie and all-round massager; ultra quiet, discreet and stylish.	No gimmicks or cool tricks.	If there's a chance airport security will be waving your vibrator around, this is the one you'd choose. "Um, that's my neck rest."	YES
Aqua Allstar	Dark blue jelly, 13cm (5 inch) long, two-branched for innie, outie and bottom play and also waterproof.	**	Like going to bed with two men at once; puts the "ahhhh" back into bath time.	Danger – slippery when wet!	Adds new meaning to the phrase, "singing in the shower".	YES
Fukouku 9000	Battery-operated, rubbery thimble that fits like an extension on the tip of your finger; comes with interchangeable textured finger pads.	*	Slides onto any finger; portable; as loud as a happy mosquito.	It pulses rather than vibrates, so not for a quickie session or for those who value their manicure.	It is guaranteed not to make any man feel inadequate!	YES
InJOY Yourself	Skin-like material, realistic looking, battery-operated, it comes with a harness and built-in suction cup.	**	Just like a real penis – the shaft moves up and down to simulate the real thrusting of sex and the balls vibrate.	There's no afterplay.	Yes, it's just like the real thing – but you're in control.	YES
Hitachi Magic Wand	30cm (12 inch) long appliance with a firm tennis-ball sized head, multi-speed and attachments available for innie use. Plug in.	**	High Richter scale vibrations and lasts forever. An industry classic.	Can be too much vibration; can sound like a freight train; it's huge; you need a steady hand and it'll freak him out.	Does the job in seconds – but you can go from tickled to numb in less than five minutes.	NO
Remote Control Alien	Battery-operated, jelly material with one setting.	**	Puts your lover in control; a toy for two; vibrations are subtle which makes it ideal for its out-and-about function, unexpected 'shocks' from your partner, works up to four metres away.	Puts your lover in control; has no instructions so it's trial and error figuring out how to work it; needs readjustment as day goes on; has only one speed.	Double the pleasure by combining it with going shopping.	NO
Wahl 7-in-1	Coil massager; seven textured heads designed for use on different massage points on the body.	***	Quieter than a Mercedes and dependable.	It looks like a hairdryer and is heavy on the wrist.	What it lacks in grace and wit, it more than makes up for in oomph.	NO

5 last answers to those questions you have about vibrators but are afraid to ask

Will using a vibrator give me an orgasm if I have never had one before?

Let's say you have more chance of having an orgasm than a space probe has of finding life on Mars. If it doesn't work for you, then try a different toy. There are hundreds of models and they all have a unique feel, power and pulse. You may feel more comfortable trying solo or you may only be successful if you share your toy with a lover.

But sexual satisfaction is more than a handful of batteries and an "on" switch. If you're thinking of buying a vibrator with the hope that your entire sexual core will open up, all it will do is give you an orgasm. It's up to you to figure out why your pocket rocket could do what no lover (and possibly your own hand) has been able to do before. Did you stimulate a different-from-usual part of your body? Was it the type or the duration or the power of the vibrations? Until you match your mechanical bliss with some hard thinking to figure out what makes you tick orgasm-wise, then the only sexual pleasure you will get is from your toy.

Many women go multiple when they have an earth-shaking climax using a vibrator.

My vibrator suddenly sounds like it's about to take off. What's going on?

The battery is probably rolling around inside. This often happens with Slimline Vibes because they're made of hard plastic and there's no insulation to stop the battery from vibrating against the hard plastic casing. Refer to the tips in "Do You Want to Make Your Neighbours Jealous?", p56.

I can't figure out where all the straps on my vibrating clitoral stimulator are supposed to go .

These things should really come with diagrams. It varies from toy to toy, but generally:

♥ If it has one long and two shorter elastic straps, wrap the longer strap around your waist and hook it to an elastic loop on the other side of the vibe. Then stretch the two smaller straps around the thighs and lock them in place with the hook to the elastic loop at the base of the strap.

♥ If there are just two elastic straps, all you need to do is change their length with the adjustable tension hooks and slides. However, on some designs, you can adjust the length first and then secure them with hooks to elastic loops at the base of the strap.

Always check out the picture on the packaging — you'll see how the straps are supposed to look once they're looped around.

62

scream machines

I masturbate sometimes with a vibrator. OK, a lot. Lately, when I have sex with my boyfriend, it feels good but I can't climax. Is it the vibrator?

Chances are it's more a case that your body knows what it likes and it doesn't seem to be getting it from your boyfriend. You may have become accustomed to a certain type of stimulation during your solo buzz offs that you're not getting in partner sex.

You can either include your vibrator in your love duets with your boyfriend (see Chapter 2 for the lowdown on how to do this and Chapter 7 for the details on what to do) or you can alter your masturbation routine to include other types of stimulation – which will expand your sensation range so that your body is more receptive to the way your boyfriend is playing with it.

You might also be climaxing so often through masturbation that when it comes to partner sex, your body doesn't really care if it goes for the gold. If you'd prefer to come the old fashioned way with your boyfriend, try cutting back on your powered masturbation and see if it makes a difference.

A battery vibe is less intense than a mains-powered one.

It's easy to go numb when you place a power wand on your clitoris and just leave it there.

Getting the right power is important when using a vibrator. Check the pressure. Since your upper lip has the equivalent number of nerve endings to a woman's vagina, that'll give you a good idea of what a vibrator will feel like to you.

What's the difference between all these rabbit vibrators?

Most are similar in the way that chocolate ice cream is similar to Dutch cocoa ice cream is similar to fudge ice cream. They're *all* ice cream and good for what ails you. Differences in rabbits include noise level, material, durability, power, texture, and where the controls are located.

Basically, if you're going for economy and don't mind a stronger smell and a slightly lower quality toy, the Jack Rabbit is for you. If you only want the best, even if it is a bit on the loud side, go with the Rabbit Pearl. If you like a slightly longer and more powerful toy, try the Techno Rabbit.

Turn on, start slow and then rev up.

You have it – now how do you start the bunny hop? To avoid ending up the wrong kind of hot and sweaty, start with the basics: take a look at your vibrator and identify the two main parts: the "shaft," which is the bit that looks like a penis, and the external "bunny" clitoral stimulator.

Next, play with the controls before you play with your toy to get a handle on what moves what and where and how it does it. Depending on the type of vibrator you have and the controller that powers it, you'll most likely be able to control two separate functions: The shaft will most likely rotate for innie pleasure and the bunny will vibrate against the clitoris for outie loving.

Slide the shaft slowly into your vagina, with the bunny facing up. You'll know you have everything inserted correctly when the bunny's ears are roughly lined up over your clitoris. If your bunny vibrator also has rotating pearls or beads in the shaft, these will probably be near your vaginal opening at this point.

What's the buzz?

These vibes are a more than a bit bizarre, but they get the job done.

The Clitoris Pump

Why you might pass on it: The small but powerful hand pump attached by a hose to a Lucite cylinder (to fit over the clitoris) looks like it would be more comfortable in a bike shop.

Why you'd be a fool to miss out: If your love button could talk it might beg you to invest in one of these – a vibrator specially designed to make it do somersaults. Three pumps and your clitoris is inflated to the size of a small rodent and super-sensitive. Switch on the built-in vibe and Badda-bing, badda-BOOM!

Think again: It's pricey, not every woman is into turning her love knob into a mini penis and the pump is so strong that overuse can create tissue damage.

Vibrating Triple Super Suck-her

Why you might pass on it: With dual nipple stimulators and a clitoris pump for triple stimulation combined with three mini-vibrators, this contraption looks like something straight out of some sci-fi nightmare.

Why you'd be a fool to miss out: it makes a woman orgasm like crazy.

Think again: It may make you feel too sexy for your shirt, but you certainly won't look it.

Masturbation Sleeve

Why you might pass on it: It's a vibrating mouth or vagina for his jacking off pleasure. It might be better at it than you.

Why you'd be a fool to miss out: He will adore you forever and at least you know what he will be up to when you are not around.

Think again: You may never see him again – these things really work! Some guys even have multiples using them. Of course, you could always pick up some tips and perfect your own style by using them with him.

Stimulation Systems' Slightest Touch Orgasmatron

Why you might pass on it: About the size of a Walkman, it works via a pair of electrical pads attached to the ankles that, when applied 10–20 minutes before sex, supposedly stimulate two acupuncture points related to your pelvic nerve pathways. Come again?

Why you'd be a fool to miss out: It's Viagra for women, taking you to a pre-orgasmic state where the "slightest touch" can trigger multiple multiples that are more intense and longer than your usual fare.

Think again: It'll blow the bank account but it doesn't actually produce orgasms – just creates a playing field for them.

www.vibelet.com's Purring Kitty

Why you might pass on it: You download this program to turn your ordinary mobile phone into a vibrating pocket rocket. Once installed, it has just two controls: Start and Pause. While running, an image of a contented cat is displayed on the phone's screen. A full charge lasts about an hour – which is how long you may need considering the low vibrations.

Why you'd be a fool to miss out: It gives new meaning to the term "phone sex".

Think again: Would you want to call your parents on a phone that you've shoved down your knickers?

Ultimate Triple Stimulator

Why you might pass on it: He slips a 15cm (6 inch) bendable jelly stimulator over his penis, making him look like something an Ork dragged in.

Why you'd be a fool to miss out: A triple treat among sex toys, it hugs the base of the penis as the vibrating bullet stimulates the penis, clitoris, vagina, and anus at the same time making it a his-and-hers multi-orgasmic toy.

Think again: You're bound to get jealous over who the new toy is giving more attention to.

Fukuoku Five Finger Massage Glove

Why you might pass on it: A glove with a tiny vibrator in every fingertip, this is no high fashion accessory.

Why you'd be a fool to miss out: At 45,000 vibrations per minute, it's the ultimate in total body stimulation.

Think again: Don't – buy it!

Tongue Vibrator

Why you might pass on it: They look like road kill in various states of decomposition. The Fun Tongue, The Tongue, Tongue II, Tongue Joy are all battery-operated, mini vibes that flick your clitoris like a tongue – some can even be worn in the mouth.

Why you'd be a fool to miss out: The sensation feels exactly like oral sex – for you and him.

Think again: For a tongue, it's awfully noisy and unless it's made of silicone, forget it as it will feel downright icky.

Tipbit
Use lots of lube to make it feel more like the real thing.

Ticklingbra

Why you might pass on it: Two jelly pads, each with its own multi-speed vibrator for underneath your own bra, giving you an instant Pamela Anderson makeover.

Why you'd be a fool to miss out: If your breasts are one of your favourite hot spots, this will give them non-stop loving attention.

Think again: Do you really want jiggly jugs?

Nipple Vibrator

Why you might pass on it: A mini vibe just for the nipples seems like an extravagance and a lot of unnecessary hooplah.

Why you'd be a fool to miss out: You can discover just how responsive every inch of your skin is to touch and vibration with these micro vibes. And because they're low-powered, you can also give his bits and bobs a buzz without electrifying them (in a bad way) as well as break the monotony with a sneak attack on your clitoris. Some clamp on to your nipples for a constant kick.

Think again: Any multi-speed vibe set on low will have the same effect.

Vibrating Cock Ring

Why you might pass on it: A ring that fits around his penis and vibrates sounds like he gets all the fun. Plus many are adorned with creatures that, when put in place, look like they are chomping on his penis the way a squirrel devours a corn on the cob.

Why you'd be a fool to miss out: Actually, the vibe is for you – he only gets a slight buzz around the base of his penis.

Think again: It takes a lot of manoeuvring to get the vibes where you want them. Of course, all the squirming around on his stick could be a lot of fun too.

Because they're not intended for prolonged use, extended love sessions may cause the motor in a handheld fan to overheat or the batteries to drain quickly.

THE CHEAPSKATE'S GUIDE TO VIBRATING
Ten ways to buzz without buying:

- Jet off in a whirlpool. Get closer to the jet for more intense stimulation, and back away when you want a lighter touch.
- No jets in your tub? Position your pelvis underneath the tub spout and run a stream of warm (not too hot!) water. Spread your lips slightly apart and let the sensation take you away.
- Strategically position your shower head (or get a hand-held shower).
- Hop on your washing machine during the spin cycle.
- Put your pager or phone on vibe and put in place.
- Turn the gear stick in your car into a joy stick.
- Take off your pants and go for a ride on a motorcycle.
- Invest in an electric toothbrush. You can use them as a vibrator with or without the brush attachment (but if you do use the brush, don't skimp – buy a separate one to set aside).
- Look for video game controllers with vibrating units.
- Use the back end of a personal handheld fan.

Create a more comfortable wand by slipping a piece of flexible rubber hose or tubing over the brush.

Don't use any vibrator designed to deliver heat to the body as a sex toy — they're great for muscles but they could singe your tenderer bits.

67

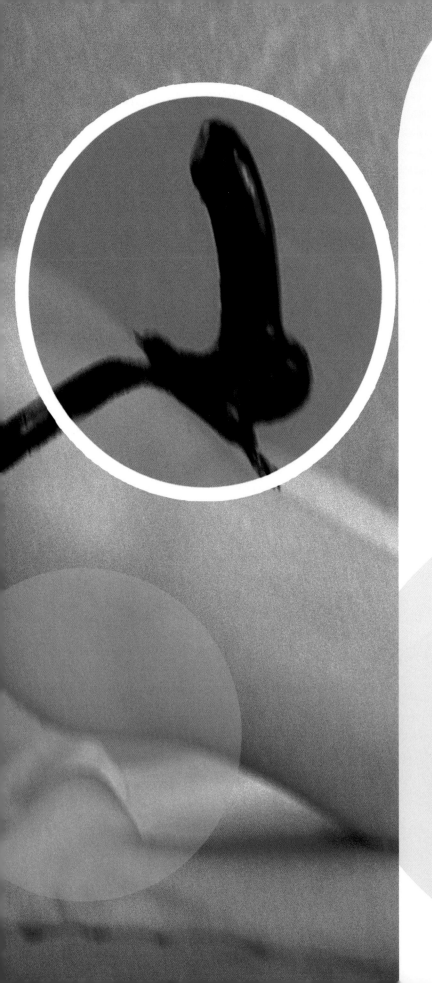

CHAPTER 6
ding, dang, dong!

Is that a dildo in your pocket or are you just happy to see me?

Mostly, **dildos** resemble men's penises, but sometimes they come in **DIFFERENT COLOURS** and with **way-too-weird gadget-like** guises like spikes and pointed tips. You can understand why people might want to give those a miss, but you have to ask: why would anyone want to use a dildo at all? They don't vibrate. They don't twist. They don't rock-n-roll. They're not even self-powered.

Actually, dildos have a lot of surprising uses. You can use a dildo as...

A sub mid-game: some penises just don't have the staying power to play a full game, let alone keep it up if you go into overtime. That's where dildos come in – literally. If the man loses it early in the match, or even if the woman can simply outlast her lover, he can continue to penetrate her with the dildo. It gives him time to recharge his batteries and keeps her aroused. So when he's ready to come back in, there's still some interest on the playing field.

A way to let him know you love him for his mind: when you whip out that ten-incher, any illusions he has about you adoring his best friend will be demolished.

A way to keep the vagina in prime condition: think of a dildo as just another type of Nautilus. The more you insert one, the more you are working your vaginal muscles and keeping them strong.

A cigarette holder or paperweight: some dildos look like anything but and can be put to various unexpected uses around the house.

To get two for one: using a dildo means you can get oral sex and be penetrated at the same time.

A safe one-night stand: you're in the mood for a little nookie with no willing and able man in sight. What could be better than using a dildo? You know it won't give you an infection, a pregnancy or make an excuse to leave in the middle of the night.

A little self awareness therapy: you can use it alone to figure out what kind of penetration you like best without having to deal with the anxiety of your lover hovering and asking, "Do you like this? What about that?" as he pokes you like a pincushion.

A sure thing. A dildo will never turn you down or tire out. You can use it whenever you want for as long as you want. The only downer is it doesn't cuddle after, but then again, it can't complain either.

TOP OF THE POPS

There are so many different types of dildos out there, how can you tell whether what looks attractive on the shelf will be great for you once you get it home or an embarrassing story waiting to happen? By going for your type:

If you are into **BELTS**: wear a dildo (see p.73 for more on why you would want to wear one in the first place), you insert it through a hole in a harness. The harness is then strapped to the user.

But make sure your dildo measures up if you're planning to harness it – it needs to be at least six inches long and have a flared or flat unbendable base or it may slip out.

Also consider the angle: Dildos that are curved will arc up and away from the body when worn in a harness. If the dildo is straight, it will aim toward the floorboards, owing both to gravity and to the slightly downward title of the pelvis. For that reason, stiff dildos with a curve tend to look better and are easier to control (without a hand guiding it to its destination).

Rating: ✳✳✳

Best of the bunch: Cyberskin™ Strap-on Dark, Silicone Buzz, Vac-U-Lock (this harness comes with a "plug" which accepts specially designed dildos that have a hole

Any borderline dildos, like the smaller Hot Rods and Silks, can be used with a smaller O-ring (if you have a harness with an adjustable O-ring, like the Terra Firma)

Chill out: try sticking a glass dildo in the fridge for an hour before use.

at the base. The vacuum created when the plug is inserted into the hole is enough to keep the dildo in place).

If you want something that doubles as a cheap objet d'art: **GLASS AND ACRYLIC DILDOS** are often very beautiful but also slick and durable (a good thing, considering where you'll be sticking them).

Rating: ✳✳✳

Best of the bunch: Mantric's Art Elite, Moon & Stars Spiral series, 7-Inch Amber, 7-Inch Worked Head Wand, Glass Massage Wand series.

Toys with balls will need specific harnesses that can accommodate them.

If you want the occasional fill-in penis without the body attached: go for a **REALISTIC DILDO** – these are shaped, sized and coloured to match a real penis (attention celebrity hounds – they're sometimes cast from a fabulous famous porn star's well-endowed anatomy) and made of a material that actually feels like skin. Some even have veins and squeezable balls! And just like your average erect member, they're rigid but still flexible, with the outside moving and wrinkling like skin. However, these babies never droop.

Rating: ✳✳

Best of the bunch: Cyber Cock, Cyberskin™ Dream, Emperor 6-Inch Dildo, Emperor 8-Inch Dildo, Raging Realistic, Soft Touch, Ultraskin 6-Inch,

Vac-U-Lock 6-Inch Dildo, Natural 6-Inch, Jeff Stryker Realistic, Trueskin Hunk.

If you aren't into DIY penises: most dildos have at least the hint of a penis shape. But some are made to be reminiscent of a penis without being realistic. Others take that idea one step further. It seems logical that if one curve works, than two or three would be even better. Silicone gives the best choices when you want **SOMETHING OUTSIDE THE BOX** – or rather, the tube.

Rating: ✳✳✳

Best of the bunch: Sirens series, Stimulator, Bobbie Sue, Treasure Chest

If you want to turn it into a **HAT HOOK**: some dildos come with suction cup-style bases that allow them to be secured to smooth surfaces – such as a tiled surface – for stand-up fun.

Rating: ✳

Best of the bunch: Extra Thick Solid Cock, Mr Big, Ultraskin, Big Red, Emperor.

If you don't mind if it's **INFLEXIBLE**: after all, it's not like you're going to argue with it. Plastic dildos generally have hard, smooth, stiff exteriors.

Rating: ✳

Most popular plastic dildos: Seaside Pleasure Pearls, Emperor series.

If you want to cuddle up with it at night:

go with a **SKIN-LIKE MATERIAL** (see Material Girl, pp.22–5). It's smooth, soft, flexible, and feels very similar to skin.

Rating: ✳✳✳

Best of the bunch: Cyber Cock, Cyberskin™ Dream, Raging Realistic, Vac-U-Lock 6-Inch Dildo.

If you want to have a threesome with your lover: go with **SILICONE** – it can be disinfected between people.

Rating: ✳✳✳

Best of the bunch: Silicone Buzz, Silicone Twist.

If you want two for the price of one: a **DOUBLE-HEADED DILDO** can be used at both ends. It's like going to bed with two men at once (since most doubles are made of jelly, make sure you read Chapter 4 if you share it).

Rating: ✳✳

Best of the bunch: 12-Inch Veined Gel Double, Double Header Dong, Jelly Double Dong Flesh, Double Delight Dildo, 12-Inch Smooth or Veined Translucent Double, Feeldoe, Nexus Jr.

If you want to press your **G-SPOT** in ten seconds or less: these have all right curves to make you go, "G-g-g-oh!"

RATING: ✳✳

BEST OF THE BUNCH: Wavy G, Crystal Wand.

If you are into heavy metal: **METAL DILDOS** are similar to plastic ones, in that they have a hard, generally smooth exterior. Think power tool without the gadgets.

RATING: *

BEST OF THE BUNCH: Heavy Metal Ribbed Handle/Shaft.

Double-headed dildos tend to be around 38 cm (15 inches) long; definitely not for beginners.

If you want back-door entry: you'll need to make sure the dildo is specifically designed for **ANAL** use with a flared base or cord so it doesn't get lost in your bottom nether regions.

RATING: **

BEST OF THE BUNCH: Anal Exciter, Anal Retriever.

If you don't have a clue what you want: one word – **LATEX**. It doesn't last as long as the other materials but it's cheaper and a wide variety of dildo types are made from it, so you can experiment pretty easily.

Some people have an allergic reaction to latex. If you're one of them, try jelly as it also is on the less pricey side.

RATING: *

BEST OF THE BUNCH: Classic, Emperor 8" Dildo, Hard & Erect.

RATINGS:

*: It might put a smile on your face under the right circumstances

** : It'll roll your socks off

***: Get ready to wake the neighbours

SEXESSORIZE

It's all in the extras.

Electric vibrators: Add a buzz by holding an electric vibe against the base of a dildo once you've slipped it in – bullets are best as they can be worn in a dildo or a harness (see Chapter 5).

Coupler: Turns any two common-or-garden variety dildos with bases into a custom-made double dildo.

Harness Cuff: Wrap it around the straps of any harness (except the Crown) to hold a second toy inside the harness wearer's opening of choice.

Slip Not or Black Rubber O Rings: Some dildos have an embarrassing tendency to skid across the floor when you harness them in. These must-have devices anchor them in place (and the Slip Not adds some extra cushioning in case of a bumpy ride).

Night Rider: Lets you strap it on pretty much anywhere from a motorcycle seat or your work chair (your boss will wonder why you're so happy at work) to over a door or onto your back or your thigh.

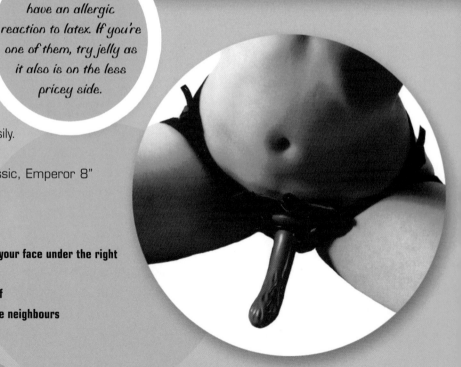

Driver Pad: Prolonged or vigorous thrusting with a harness can give you bruises – this is the perfect shape to cushion your pubic bone.

Lubrication: Absolutely necessary if you plan to use your dildo for inner exploration (see Chapter 3 for more info).

Strap-On Harnesses: The image that probably springs to mind is girl-on-girl scenes in porn videos. But strap-ons can be fun for everyone. A strap-on is basically a sex-toy combo that includes a dildo attached to a harness that is worn around the waist or hips. The harness has a triangular or rectangular front piece that sits over a woman's vulva or the base of a man's penis, and the front piece has a special opening or O-ring through which you can slip a special dildo with a flared, flat-bottom base. This gives women an artificial penis right where one should hang, or, in the case of men, provides an extra penis right below his own.

Mix and match to find the harness style that suits you (see Tools of the Trade p.21 for info on harness materials).

STYLE **Thong or one strap:** One strap circles the waist or hips and the other strap connects to the base of the front piece then runs between the wearer's legs, up through the butt cheeks (like a thong), attaching to the waist/hip strap in back.
STRAP IT ON Fewer straps which means fewer strap adjustments; the straps rub your love zone, it looks sexy, it's unlikely to slip.
TAKE IT OFF The strap rubbing your love zone means he can't and it may feel like you have a wedgie.

STYLE **Jock:** one strap circles the waist or hips and attaches to the front piece. Two other straps attach to the base or sides of the front piece and circle each of the wearer's thighs, attaching to the waist/hip strap in back.
STRAP IT ON The extra strap means the dildo won't unexpectedly droop and the wearer's most sensitive bits are left wide open.
TAKE IT OFF The style can make you self-conscious of your buns.

STYLE **Panty:** exactly what it sounds like, with a hole for a dildo to poke through.
STRAP IT ON Usually made of latex.
TAKE IT OFF Some people are allergic to latex. Panties are uncomfortable for men, holding their genitals too tightly. They're not great at holding the weight of anything but the smallest dildo.

STYLE **Thigh harness:** straps to your thigh
STRAP IT ON Gives you the extra thrusting power of those awesome quadriceps you built up on that damn stair-stepper, great for sitting-up sex; good for simultaneous push-me-pull-me penetrative sex; a must for anyone with hip problems.
TAKE IT OFF Can be fiddly to get exact height right (mark the skin in permanent marker when you do!).

A harness with a buckle means it won't loosen on you at the wrong yes-oh-yes moment.

73

5 last answers to those questions you have about dildos but are afraid to ask

My boyfriend wants me to use a dildo on him – does this mean he's really gay?

Only if his lifelong dream is to have brunch with Barbra, Liza and Kylie (and even then, he may just have a select musical taste). The only given about gay men and dildos is that there is none. Sexual orientation – straight, gay or bisexual – has less than zero to do with the kinds of sex acts you enjoy. The bottom is just another e-zone and many men who are 100 per cent heterosexual enjoy having their anus massaged, fingered and penetrated – including penetration with strap-ons. Guys even have a hotspot just inside their rectum called the prostate gland. It sounds like your boyfriend is one of those rare finds: someone who knows what he likes sexually and isn't afraid to ask for it.

Does size matter when it comes to dildos?

Actually, diameter is even more important that length. Length is less important as you can always control the depth of thrusting.

Dildos used in harnesses are going to end up being up to 2.5cm (1 inch) shorter because of the space taken up by the harness.

However, you can't make something

When in doubt, go smaller – just like the eyes are bigger than the stomach phenomenon that happens at buffets, it's easy to choose too much. A toy that's too big is useless but a toy that's a touch small can still make for a pretty good time. Also, choose a dildo that starts small at the top and gradually widens in thickness to the base – it will be easier to work in.

that feels like it's tearing you apart smaller. So choose a dildo with the approximate girth of the number of fingers you would like inside of you or about the size of a penis you've loved in the past. If you're not sure, peel a large cucumber and try inserting it (lie down first). Keep carving the cuke down until you are at a size that feels comfortable. Voilà: you have your ideal dildo width!

If you're on the small side, you can always trim a harness down to fit.

I'm on the large size – do harnesses come in different sizes?

Sizing on harnesses is pretty basic. All the nylon harnesses are one size only and fit up to about a 46–48 inch hip. Most of the leather harnesses come in one size as well (about a 44 inch hip), but you can order an extra long backstrap (about 54 inches total) for the

74

harnesses that have D-ring fasteners. The Terra Firma is the only one that comes in two sizes: regular (44 inch hip) and large (54 inch hip). The Crown harness (54 inches around at the top) is made to fit higher on your belly so that you can have the dildo out where you need it.

The thing to remember about these measurements is that it depends on where you wear your harness. If you wear it a bit high on the curve toward your waist, you'll be left with room in the strap. So if you decide to measure for fit, measure where you are going to want that top strap to run.

I just bought a dildo and it's so stiff it almost hurts when I use it. Is this how it's supposed to feel?

If it's plastic, this is what you are stuck with – you may want to think about a more realistic material (see Material Girl, pp. 22–5). Otherwise, you probably have a rubber dildo. These do become more flexible with time. To make it soft in a hurry (the opposite of what you would want in a willy!), leave it in the sun for a while, however, you might want to make sure you've left it in a place that can't be seen by neighbours or your kids!

My dog found my dildo. I managed to get it away before he did too much damage – there are only a few bite marks. It's silicone, so can I revive it by just boiling it?

Why would you want to? Yes, silicone is

Don't get any bright ideas and nuke your rubber dildo in the microwave to soften it up. You may end up cooking it from the inside out and end up burning yourself when you use it.

expensive. And yes, you can sterilize it by boiling it. But putting aside the yuck factor of intimately sharing a toy with your dog, the silicone may have a small tear or crack that will break apart as soon as you put any pressure on it. And if you think having your dog chew up your dildo is embarrassing, try going to A&E with a dildo stuck in your vagina.

See Chapter 1 for info on how to store your toys safely and discreetly.

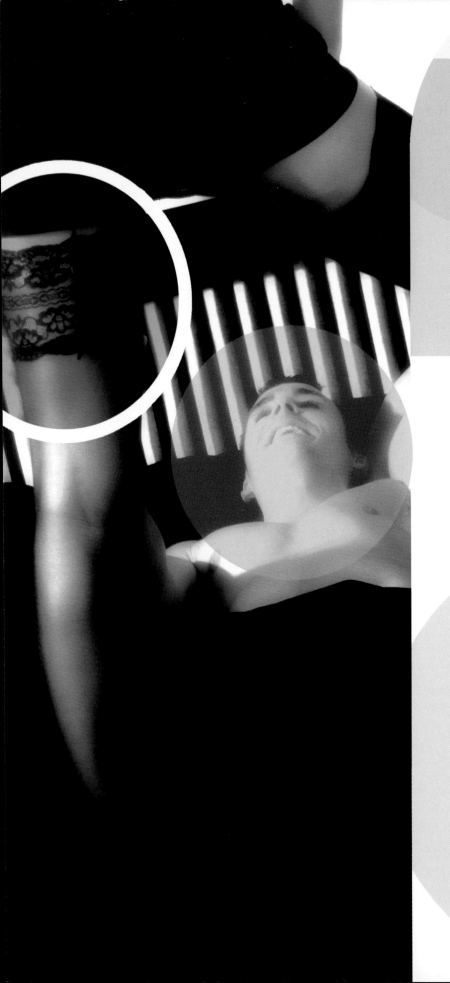

CHAPTER 7
sexpertise

Hurrah! You have your new toy in hand. Only thing is, you may be asking, "What the hell do I do with it?" Not an unreasonable question when you consider that some vibrators and dildos look more like pet toys or bedside lights than anything you would put on your body's most intimate parts. The fact that many come with no directions doesn't help, either.

Here are plenty of tips and techniques to help you and your lover – should you be so inclined to let him in on the fun – have the best orgasms ever.

Make nice and play

Warning: You may need a spatula.

Beginner's Moves

Key

D: This move will be more orgasmic when used with a dildo

V : This move will be more orgasmic when used with a vibe

* Do this when you want to have fun on your own

- The day you get the toy, make a night out of it. Light some candles and switch on a romantic tune. Rip open the box together. Both of you play with it, trying it out on your bodies while you're still dressed, slowly warming each other up. Get undressed and rub it against your genitals. If it's a penetrative toy, slowly slip it in and leave it in for a moment. Don't start thrusting crazily. Switch between his tool and your new one. Make sure you're using his for the finale so he feels comfortable (translation: your new toy is not a very successful sub for him). D,V

- Get in the mood. Read/watch a favourite passage from a sexy book/movie (see Resources for ideas). When you feel aroused, stop and replay the scene in your head while using your new toy for stimulation all the way to orgasm. D, V *

- Start with a light massage. Light some candles, then rub the vibrator over your arms, breasts and tummy. Slowly stroke your legs, working upward toward your bottom and saving your love zone for last. V *

- Build slowly to release. Get close to the brink, then back away to step up the pleasure. D, V *

Make sure you have your lube handy because once play starts getting serious, you won't want to stop to hunt for it.

Basic rules

1. Start slow. Save the double dong or 30cm (12 inch) vibrator for once you have a few toy encounters notched on to your belt. Try a nice, simple rocket vibrator or classic dildo to begin with. Once you and your sweetie are in a good comfort zone, you can trade up.

2. Take your time. Block out a few hours or a whole evening, afternoon or whatever. Getting to know your new vibe or dildo is not something you can do in an hour (although you can certainly send yourself into an orgasmic tizzy in that time). You need the time to explore your body with it to find out what you like.

3. You don't have to use your toy during actual intercourse unless you want to. Instead, plan a "play date" to get warmed up and then toss the toy when he's ready to climb aboard.

4. Put the brakes on the first few times you play with toys. You don't have to see everything it can do the first time you test drive it. There's plenty of time to accelerate!

5. Talk, talk and talk to each other. You may both have sealed the deal to use a toy, but that doesn't mean that once the action is going down, you both feel as comfortable as you did when you were just kicking the idea around. Make sure you are both as happy as clams. If not, you need to put the toy back in its box and decide if you want to continue.

6. If the answer to Rule #5 is thumbs down, try a new course. The toy you've selected might turn out to be totally wrong for your sexual personalities. That's okay. Put it aside and try something different.

7. If the answer to Rule #5 is still no, it does not mean that the toy should be binned. The half of your duet that was still singing happily should be able to give it a solo go if they desire.

8. Use lubrication (see Chapter 3). Sex toys need lots of lube to slip and slide the way they should. Make sure you lube up your genitals and the vibe or dildo, especially if it's a penetrative one.

Most women climax in 60 seconds to three minutes when they use a vibrator so as tempting as it is, keep backing away from your clitoris or whatever your favourite send-off point is.

• Don't limit yourself to the major erogenous zones. The entire body is chock-full of tingling nerves, just waiting to be given a caress. The thinner the skin in the area you are touching, the more responsive it will be. Try rubbing your toy along the neck, tummy, inner thighs, inner forearms and temples for some out-of-this-world sensations. D, V *

• Explore your outer areas. Lie on your back, spread your legs, and lightly caress your outer vaginal lips with vibrator. This is an extremely sensitive erogenous zone that's often ignored. Lightly stroke the area for several minutes. Then explore your inner lips. Rub and stroke on or around your clitoris until you detonate. V *

• Bring yourself to the brink with your fingers, then insert a dildo before your finale. As your vaginal muscles spasm, they contract against the dildo, adding pressure – and ecstasy. D *

• Set your tool on the lowest speed, applying light, circular pressure to your clitoris. Keep it where it is when you're ready to roll. V *

• Some women find direct clitoral stimulation too intense so work around the bump. V *

• Have your lover rub little circles around your love button with a vibrator while he licks your breasts and belly. Three words: Oh. My. God. V

• If you have a G-spot vibe (see Chapter 5), experiment with twisting it around in your vagina to hit all the inner different spots (see tipbit, right). V *

• If you like it deep inside of you, go for your G-spot as opposed to going in and out with the vibrator. D, V *

• Don't limit yourself to one stroke. Sure it may work, but it will also get you stuck in a rut. Try a circular motion, a back-and-forth rhythm, an in-and-out thrust deep and then shallow – play around until you find a few moves that wow you. D, V *

• If it's a penetrative vibe or dildo, insert it into your vagina. Wiggle it around in there. Try different depths. Hold it just at the opening of the vagina. If there's a larger head at the tip of the vibrator, try very shallow dips with just the tip. D, V *

- Don't forget to use your hands, tongue and/or other toys to add to the love fest. If you have an external vibe, penetrate your vagina with your fingers. Rub your anus, stroke his penis, squeeze your nipples, rub your vaginal lips, squeeze his testicles. Work it all over. V *

- Have him bring in a stunt double – he uses his tongue on your love knob as he slowly inserts the sex toy inside of you. D, V *

- Sometimes, a little bathroom time is the only time you are going to get to yourself. The only drawback is that partner play can be limited if you don't have a big space. However, there are ways to get around a tiny tub. Begin with him washing your hair (body-melting foreplay). He can then sit by the tub and arouse you with your (waterproof!) vibe while you soak. V

- Another water trick is to change the temperature while caressing each other with the vibrator, switching taps from seductively hot to shockingly cold, and then back to hot again. The stimulation of the temperature, along with the vibrator, can be intense. V

- If you have private access to a pool, hot tub or ocean, try playing Triple XXX Marco Polo with your partner. Close your eyes while your partner swims around you. When you call "Marco!", your partner responds with "Polo!" Once you locate your partner, he rewards you with a touch from a waterproof vibrating toy. V

- Press your toy against the perineum, the small area between your vagina/his testicles and the anus, for an unexpected pleasure buzz. Bonus: you'll also thrill his prostate (the male G-spot) with this move. V *

- Give your bottom a buzz. Lie on your belly with a pillow positioned under your hip bones, then reach back and stimulate your vagina and clitoris from behind. V *

- Try running the vibrator on a low setting down the shaft of his penis. V

- Instead of lying on your back and applying the toy, switch the action and lay directly on your sex toy. D, V *

- Straddle the vibe/dildo. D, V *

- Put the vibe on your genitals and squeeze your thighs and bottom cheeks together, then release. Repeat until you detonate. V *

In chemically treated and salt waters, jelly and toys crafted from "lifelike" materials die quickly, so it might be better to stick to slimline plastic massagers, pocket rockets or vibrating sponges, all of which are more resilient to harsh chemicals (and slightly less expensive!).

Remember the ocean has waves. If you don't want to lose your toy, you might want to anchor it with a wrist strap.

Pro Moves

- Variety is the spice to life. While your single toy may get the job done, the more you branch out, the more chances at pleasure you are going to have (see Sexessorize in Chapter 5 p.59 and Chapter 6, p.72, for some ways to dress up your sex toy). We dress according to our moods, so why shouldn't we also play according to our moods? D, V *

- One favourite combo is to use an outie vibe to stimulate the clitoris during intercourse and to use an innie vibe during mutual masturbation (see pp.60–61, for vibrator choices). V *

- Orgasm without your partner (or even yourself for that matter) ever even touching you. Even when you're out in public. Vibrating panties or wireless, wearable clitoral stimulators make it easy to leave the bedroom (see p.58, for suggestions). V *

- Try doing it doggie style while having him doubly stimulate you by gently rubbing the vibrator across your love bump as he enters you. V

- If it gets too hot in your bedroom, cool things off by turning your toy into a chilly popsicle. Stick a waterproof vibrator or a glass or acrylic dildo in the freezer for an hour then take it out and tickle your lover's fancy with it. For an even greater thrill, keep another waterproof vibrator or glass or acrylic

dildo in a bowl of warm water by the bed, then switch between using the cold and the warm toys. D, V *

- Raise the temperature a notch on the above by having your lover tie you down (see pp.116–9 for how-tos). He can use one of the toys to penetrate you and the other to play with your nipples, breasts, neck, etc. D, V

- Take the above tip into a deeper arena by including anal play in your games – put the hot toy in one orifice and the cold one in the other. D, V, *

- Hit your G-spot every time – even if your toy doesn't have a special notch. Slide your toy in from behind at a slight downward angle so that it hits the front wall of your vagina in just – ahhh – the right place. D, V *

Care must be taken with the temperatures in order to avoid either burns or frostbite.

- Electrify your G-spot. Using a special G-spot vibrator, which is only a few inches long and has a slightly arched tip (see Chapter 5, p.52, for best buys), insert it with the curved side pointing toward your belly button and move it gently in a circular motion, thrusting slightly as if you were having intercourse. V *

- If you're an anal beginner, try this: Lie on your back with your bottom propped up on pillows. Use lots of lubrication (see Chapter 3) and go slowly (if you're doing this with your lover, verbally guide him as to when to push the toy and when to wait). Make sure your clitoris gets plenty of loving attention throughout to keep things loose-y juicy. D, V *

> *Make sure your toy is made for anal play (see p.57)*

- Another backward move to try is cervical stimulation. Kneel on the edge of the bed and push your toy into your vagina from behind. This way, you get penetrated extra deeply, thrusting ever so slightly in that intense spot. The pleasurable sensation builds into an inner-body cervical orgasm. D, V *

> *Stick with a gentle pulsing vibrator when standing up or you may end up in a crumpled heap on the floor within seconds.*

- Vibrate standing up. Stand with your legs apart and move your clitoris over the vibrator in all directions. V *

- If you both love visual stimulation (porn movies get you going, for example), try this: while lying side by side, masturbate together using your toys. Or try sitting on chairs opposite each other and then go to town with your toys while you watch each other. D, V

- Bond with your toy – try restraining your partner with some fuzzy handcuffs and then blindfolding him with a silky scarf. Once you've done that, use an assortment of vibrators on his body. Maybe a mini-massager on his erogenous zones while performing oral sex on him? Or you could use a clitoral stimulator on yourself while using a vibrator on him (see Chapter 11 for more on creating restraining order). D, V

- Hold a multi-speed vibrator (see Chapter 5) against and between his testicles. Keep it on low unless you want his willy to drop off. V

Getting Hitched

Strap-ons may sound a bit too out there, but they can actually add a whole new dimension to your regular sexual routine:

- They free the hands, allowing them to be used to touch in all sorts of other delicious ways.

- They let you use your hips or thighs, giving you more power for a more intense experience (not forgetting the extra calories you'll burn off).

- They let you play dress-up – you can feel what it's like to be him without worrying whether your Mr Pokey is going to peter out before reaching the point of no return. He can fulfil his lifelong fantasy of having two penises at once (just make sure he's clear whether he wants #2 to be bigger or smaller than his home grown).

- Some babes like the feeling a harness gives without accessorizing it with a dildo – especially the thong variety. It makes them come over all sexy when worn under their everyday clothes.

That said, strap-ons are a bit more elaborate than your average turn-it-on-and-buzz sex toy, and stepping into one may feel odd. Here are the basics:

1 Take your time. The dildo needs to be fitted into the front piece and straps may need to be adjusted. Count on it feeling awkward at first.

2 Use plenty of lubricant on the dildo as well as any body part you're planning to use it on before insertion.

3 Not all dildos fit all harnesses – you may have to have a few trial runs (the shop you buy the harness from should be able to steer you in the right direction – see Resources).

4 You can put the dildo in the harness either before or after you put it on, but if you've got a buckling harness, it'll be easier to put on before you tighten the straps. Depending on how the harness fits, you may find yourself with a serious downward-pointing willy or one that's a bit more perky. Simply slip it through the hole.

There's more to it than gearing up and banging away. A strap-on is definitely not a penis, so don't expect to be able to use the same positions or angles your boy might use with his own tool:

- Make sure whoever is doing the wearing doesn't start thrusting away like a turbo engine. The person on the receiving end should be in control, slowly receiving the strap-on dildo instead of being actively penetrated.

- Strap-ons leave the wearer's hands free – make sure they use them!

- If he's wearing the harness, he might switch between inserting his erection and the strap-on dildo.

- Or he can insert his penis and strap-on dildo simultaneously into your vagina and anus if you're up for it.

- If you're strapped up, enjoy the feeling of the base of the dildo pressing against your love region.

If you find yourself missing direct hands-on clitoral love, he can reach under the front piece and let his fingers do the walking. Or loosen the straps and lift the front piece or move it aside for easy access.

5 last answers to those questions you have about playing with your toys but are afraid to ask

Is it safe to use any vibrator around my bottom or does it have to be a special kind if I don't plan to stick it in?

As long as you don't intend a rear entry, any vibrator will do (though those that have lower pulses and are a bit slimmer will feel more comfortable – see p.57 for more). However, why limit yourself? You may suddenly feel like taking a deep dive once the action starts heating up. So it's better to have the right equipment from the get go – a toy with a flared base or cord so it doesn't get lost and plenty of anal lube on hand.

Is one kind of condom better than another for a sex toy?

The only thing you may want to pay attention to is size. If your toy is bigger than average, check out Maxx, Okeido and Trojan Magnum – they all have extra length, girth or both. Prime Snugger Fit, Lifestyles Snugger and Mamba are for narrower and shorter-than-average appendages.

Even if you are just knocking at the back door, you should never then move your toy towards your front door without cleaning it first (see Chapter 4, p.44)

inch) sausages being hauled out mid-play. Go with ones that don't look like the real thing at first (see Chapter 6, p.71).

I was using my remote at work and a colleague noticed the buzz. I was so embarrassed, I didn't know what to say.

Next time – although hopefully there won't be one – say, "Oops, I forgot to take my phone off vibrate – my boss hates when it rings in the middle of meetings." Then walk away while searching your pockets/bag/belt as if you have a phone tucked there. No one will be any the wiser – and if they are, they're probably jealous.

If you're sharing your sex toy and playing in areas that need cleaning in between acts, slip a condom on your toy instead of washing it. Just slip a fresh one on as needed.

To find your G-spot, use a toy specifically made for the job (see p.52).

Where the hell is my G-spot? We tried all night to find it with a dildo.

Hope you had fun. About the size of a large pea, it can be found around 5cm (2 inches, about the length of your middle finger) up on the front wall of your vagina. Good G-spot locating positions are: squatting, kneeling, lying on your stomach and – rear entry.

Do guys prefer vibrators or dildos?

Generally, a vibrator. Dildos seem just a bit too much like the service he already provides. However, if your preference runs only to dildos, choose carefully – most men get intimidated by extra-large 30cm (12

While most remotes are usually ultra quiet, the more expensive brands are even quieter (see p.56 for suggestions).

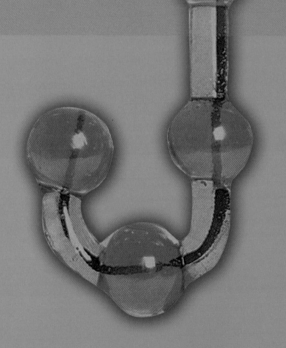

part three

toy wonders

Sex toys are so much more than vibrating bits and bobs or stand-ins for his woody. There are balls, beads, lotions, rings and all sorts of devices designed with just one thing in mind: how to get you off in the best way possible.

Granted, some are a little more weird and wacky than others – torch-shaped masturbation sleeve, anyone? But as with most things in life, there is a cover for every pot.

Read on to find yours.

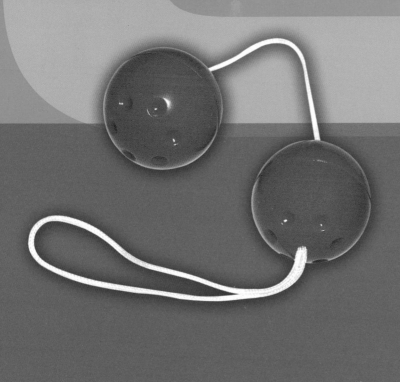

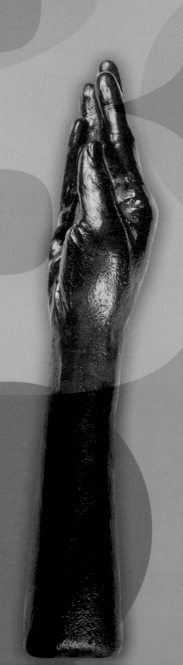

CHAPTER 8
baubles, bangles and things

A few trinkets to make you **breathe faster**.

Rating:
+ Good for a laugh
++ Check it out
+++ Must have

Beads: Think cheap kiddie necklace; beads spaced along a thin nylon cord that can be inserted vaginally or anally and then popped out right before or during orgasm (see Chapter 10, p.105, for more).
BEST BUY: Jelly Love Beads, Vaginal Anal Beads Purple.
RATING: ++

Balls: Finally, you can pack your own pair of balls. But you may decide it's not worth it. Balls are mainly for solo play – you get a pair of slightly-larger-than-children's-marbles balls in gold plating, silver, steel, plastic, Lucite or even combos of these materials. Some – like Ben Wa balls – are solid; others – like Duatones – are metal ball bearings enclosed within hollow plastic balls covered in silicone and tied together with a string or nylon cord. You stick them in the vagina like a tampon and then, while you do your shopping or go to your yoga class, the balls jiggle against each other and your insides, producing multiple orgasms. Except that your vagina keeps them firmly in place so the only way to get them to knock together is to start shaking like you are having an epileptic fit. In short, these are very expensive worry beads.
BEST BUY: Seaside Pleasure Pearls, Duatone, Triple Play.
RATING: ++ (see Tipbit below).

Liberator® Bedroom Adventure Gear™: A lot more than simple floor cushions, these pillows manipulate you into new wild positions anywhere and with anyone – no more rug burns from doing it on the floor, oral-sex crick neck and bruised shins from rear-entry slip-ups. The velvet (washable!) fabric seems to stick together so you can have some pretty heavy play without losing your position. It does take some geometric ability to figure out the best cushion arrangement for your play, but that's part of the fun.
BEST BUY: The wedge and ramp combo.
RATING: +++

If you are planning to use beads for front and back door entry, invest in two sets to keep things clean.

Balls may fizzle when it comes to creating sizzling orgasms, but they can help power up the orgasms you are having by turning them into barbells for strengthening your pubococcygeus (PC) muscle (see Kegel exerciser, p. 90). Because the balls are on the heavy side, the PC muscle must contract to keep them from sliding out. Keep them in for ten minutes at a time.

Vielle Clitoral Stimulator is like using a toothbrush down there, only a lot better. Instead of bristles, it has eight soft nubs to do the job and slips niftily over your or your lover's finger. Made from plastic, it's recommended you use one per orgasm. BEST BUY: While Vielle is a hands-down (or fingers down, rather) fave, you can use a cat toothbrush in a pinch – with 300+ nubs, they'll do the job, are cheaper and can be reused, though they do tend to slip off easily
Rating: ++

Nothing kills the mood like having your nipple ring almost ripped off your nipple with one tug! Tell him to go light on the pressure.

Nipple jewellery: If you like the pierced look but don't have the guts to get pierced, you can still have a girly moment dressing up his second favourite e-zone (after his own appendage) in a non-pierced adjustable version. Nipple rings come with crystals, sparkles, even strobe lights. They can be worn loosely for a little stimulation, or tightened for that extra squeeze. He can slightly tug on the dangling chain during foreplay (pull downward as a forward one can make the jewellery slide off). This is why you have breasts! Bonus: He tickles both nipples with one hand.
BEST BUYS: Judy's Titti Twinkler Ensemble, Nipple Teasers, Strobing NippleRings, Cleopatra's Nipple Ring Clit.
RATING: +

Some nipple rings can also double up on your love knot.

Kegel exerciser: Working your PC muscles with Kegel exercises powers up your orgasmic ability – you reach bliss more easily, experience it more explosively and can keep a tighter grip on his woody to boot. These toys are for those too lazy to Kegel themselves (see p.93). Read the instruction booklet before using! It has tips to make sure you don't waste your time or hurt yourself. You will need lots of lube to insert the exerciser. However, chances are if you couldn't be bothered to squeeze your pelvis a few times a day in the first place, having a piece of equipment is not going to turn you into a pelvic heavyweight.
BEST BUY: Kegelcisor, KegelMaster, Gyneflex, FemTone Vaginal Weights, Ben Wa Balls (see p.93).
RATING: ++

You can buff up your PCs anytime, anywhere without extra equipment. To locate your PC muscle, try stopping the flow of pee in mid-stream.

baubles, bangles & things

5 last answers to those questions you have about baubles, bangles and things but are afraid to ask

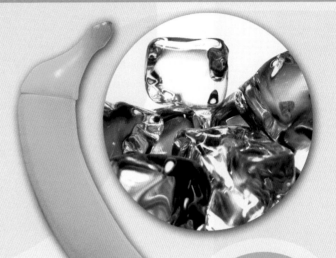

Is it safe to use a carrot as a dildo?

Definitely. Think of it as an organic sex toy. In fact, your corner shop is full of orgasmic possibilities – and not just the food aisles. Also check out the housewares department:

• Bananas, leeks, cucumbers and frozen hotdogs can all double up as dildos (but beware of freezer burn).

• Small bunches of grapes – especially if frozen first – can be used as vaginal or anal beads.

• You can use honey, chocolate syrup, jams, whipped cream or any spreadable substance to smear on your bodies for a high-calorie lick-off.

• Alternate with temperatures by adding a dollop of ice cream to your genitals and then licking it off.

• Suck a strong breath mint before oral sex.

• Candles with long wicks are especially useful wick end out – if you lose your grip the wick makes a handy retrieval method.

• A small spill of champagne over the vulva can turn it into a luxury item.

• Rub ice over your genitals to add a chill to your hot play

Don't insert anything breakable in your body – you wouldn't want it to snap mid-play.

Wash anything you are going to stick up yourself very well first or, better yet, use a condom.

• A soft rope or scarf can be tied into a DIY cock ring. Use a simple slip knot or a bow so he can slip out of it quickly in a pinch.

• Stick a ring doughnut

Unless it's supposed to be ice cold, make sure you let your home-made sex toy get to room temperature or, if possible, run it under lukewarm water to make it more comfortable to use.

91

around his penis and see how many bites it takes to eat it off.

• Take a shower and rub each other down – gently – with exfoliating gloves .

• A cardboard toilet roll can be turned into a penis sleeve.

When I used a penis pump on my boyfriend, it hurt him. Should he have been hard before we started?

Not an issue. Because the vacuum pump is drawing blood into the penis, it will work equally well whether he's in the groove or not. That said, some men find it easier to enter the pump if they're already erect.

As for his moment of pain, there are five possibilities:

1 You may not have used enough lube. You need to smear it around the entire area to keep his skin moist as prevent it from sticking to the sides of the cylinder as you pump.

2 He may have needed a trim first – his hair may have been caught and pulled as the air was sucked out to create a vacuum.

3 You may have pumped too quickly – think of how a tyre inflates. Too much air and it pops. While his penis is obviously not going to burst like a balloon, it can still feel like it is. The key to successful pumping is to go slowly.

4 He stroked his penis with a pump – this could cause some smarting if his penis hits the hard plastic of the pump at the wrong angle.

5 He may have a medical condition. He should not pump if he bleeds easily or has a blood clotting disorder, is diabetic, if he suffers from any peripheral vascular disease, or if he's taking anticoagulants, aspirin, or any other blood-thinning medication. If he experiences bruising, pain, bleeding or loss of sensation, he needs to get to a doctor ASAP.

I got my boyfriend a cock ring for his birthday. He liked it, I liked it – but then we couldn't get it off!

Talk about being stuck between a rock and a hard place! It sounds like you got him a chrome or acrylic cock ring – bad choice (as you have obviously figured out for yourself) since they don't bend and are hard to get off – and on, for that matter. To get unstuck, you need to bring his woody down – fast. The best thing to do is pack him in ice. Then use loads of lube to keep things as slippery as possible. Next time try a rubber or strap-on cock ring. These are easy to snap on and off.

Cock rings are not for diabetics, or people with any blood disorders.

Cock rings are designed to be used for 20 minutes at a time maximum. If it becomes uncomfortable remove it immediately. And he should never, ever conk out with one on or his penis may fall off (or at least hurt – a lot).

Although the flexibility of rubber and other elasticized cock rings allows a greater range of fit for more differently endowed men, no cock ring is one-size-fits-all so the right size needs to be chosen for a proper fit. To figure out his penis girth, see how many of your fingers bunched together equal the thickness of his fleshy friend when he's hard and again when he's soft and get something that fits the amount of fingers that fall in the middle of those two measurements.

Cock rings also require some finesse to get on: you need to get the ring to sit at the base of the penis, behind the scrotum – which means you have to get his balls and penis through the ring before he is standing to attention – and hopefully he won't start getting perky as you manhandle his member into place. It is possible to do it with an erect penis, but it takes some practice.

Start by slicking him up with lube. Then place the first testicle through the ring, followed by the second one. Follow by pulling the flaccid penis through the ring. The fit should be snug, but not too tight. Once he's up and ready, the fit should be about the same, if not a bit snugger, to restrict the blood flow from Mr Stiffy back into the body.

Of course, again this is all a lot easier if you're using a leather snap-on or the "tie" variety because all you have to do then is simply snap or tie it into place.

How can I get my Ben Wa balls to stay in? They seem to fall out whenever I sneeze, laugh or just move too much – very embarrassing!

These are not the easiest thing in the world to insert in the first place. To stick them in so they stay put may very well be an impossible task. The main problem is that they are round, making it difficult to actually hold in place while pushing them inside – especially if you apply lube first. The trick is to put a dab of lubricant on to yourself rather than smearing it on the toy. Once in place, the muscular ring near the outside of your vagina is supposed to hold them in place (this is the area the balls are supposed to do a cha-cha on).

However, if yours keep popping out, it may be that you need to stick them in deeper. Careful you don't go too deep though or you may hit your cervix – not dangerous, but possibly painful.

When I use my Kegel exerciser, it makes me hot – is this normal?

Absolutely – but also potentially painful if you don't stop before you orgasm. Most Kegel exercisers work on the lever principle – which means they have to be squeezed shut when you insert them or take them out. Your contractions could end up pushing the exerciser out while it is in wide-open operating mode, leaving you very sore and unfit for anything.

Boy toys

Toys specifically designed to wham, bam him.

Cock Rings: Used to make his erection harder, bigger and longer lasting, these toys work by constricting blood flow, keeping blood in the shaft of the penis instead of flowing back into his body. The rings can be made of anything from metal and acrylic to the more bendy silicone and latex or even leather or denim decked out in studs for your twisting pleasure. The best for beginners are either stretchy or strap-on and adjustable (and therefore, also easily removable should he be getting too much of a good thing).

BEST BUYS: 3 Snap Leather Ring, Tickler, Gummy Bear Ring, Techno Lover, Pleasure Rings, Romeo Rings, Neoprene Cock Ring.
RATING +

Some cock rings have built-in vibrators (see p.67).

Dipping his dick in lube will make masturbation sleeves slide on like they were custom-made for him.

Masturbation sleeves: The ultimate guy gadget, masturbators or penis sleeves are designed to stand in for a vagina or mouth when he's in the mood for some solo play. The more lifelike the material, the better the feel for him (see Chapter 1, p.23). Some are manually operated, others take all the pain out of it for him and vibrate using batteries (see Chapter 5, p.59 for more).
BEST BUYS: Hot Lips, Sex In A Can, Cyberskin Pussy, Robo-Blo, Tiger Tail Ale With Pink Mouth Orifice.
RATING: +++

Avoid using rubber bands, binder clips, and vices — they may seem like a cheap alternative, but they can cause too much restriction.

You might want to make a sexy sesh of trimming the hairs around his scrotum so that they don't get caught and pulled by snaps, locks or sticky rubber.

94

Penis pump: It's a pump. For his penis. Not attractive. It's a hollow cylinder, typically made of clear plastic or glass that is completely open at one end and has a valve or tube connected to the other end. The tube is connected to a bulb or some other mechanism by which the air can be drawn out of the cylinder after the penis is inserted, creating a vacuum.

Designed to help men whose erections are not all they could be strength-wise, a pump can't make a man hard – it can only help him to get hard or stay hard if his hot rod is already on the track.

BEST BUYS: Xtreme Sport Pump, Fireman, Power Grip Penis Pump, Millennium Pump, Power Man 6000, Cyberskin™ Pump.

RATING: +

Penis extender: These sleeves are designed to fit over his not-so-big boy, adding girth of as much as 13cm (5 inches). Some have knobs at the end designed to hit your G-spot. This is one toy where it's worth springing for the more lifelike material (see Chapter 1, p.23) as you don't want to feel like you are being stuck with a plastic loo roll holder.

BEST BUY: G-spot Extension, Cyberskin™ Extension 3, Cyberskin™ Transformer.

RATING: +

Add only a dab of lube to his penis before slipping on the extender — use too much and he'll end up sliding all over the place.

A pump won't help if either of you are underwhelmed with his main-digit measurements — after pumping, the penis will return to its regular size.

Throw a cock ring into the mix immediately after pumping to make the stiffening effect last.

If the extender is too long, you can easily trim the toy to fit his penis better. Have him slip it on and use a felt-tip marker to mark the spot on the extender to which you'd like to trim it. Remove the extender before cutting with a pair of strong scissors or you may end up giving him a trim.

Make sure the extender is a comfortable fit. If the tip of the penis is too close, it will feel crushed; too far and the extender will bend inside you during intercourse — ouch!

CHAPTER 9

lotions and potions

A lubricant is not a lubricant is not a lubricant. There are lubes to flavour your **sex play**, HEAT IT UP, **extend it**, romance things or end things quickly. Of course, if you don't use them right, they can also stain your sheets, make your hands slimy, turn your love mesh into a **greasy fiasco** where you can barely hold on to each other let along make genital contact, cause your head pound from the strong scents and destroy your contraception. Here's how to keep it **SLIPPERY** and **SAFE**.

When you want to boost your O: There are loads of pleasure-extenders on the market. Most of them are snake oil, but some topical gels actually work like arousal on crack. When applied to the love regions, they open up the blood vessels and get blood pumping to the area. They are often flavoured with mint or cinnamon to add to the tingly sensations.
Smear it on: Vigel, Orgasm Booster, Sensations Erotic Balm.

When you want to feel like a virgin, touched for the very first time:
Use a cream that tightens up the skin around the opening.
Freshen it up: Sure Grip Tighten-up Cream.

When you want to dust yourself off: Body dusts work like a light coating of talc that you sprinkle on to and then rub into your bodies to make things silky smooth. And unlike their grease-cousins, there's no oil slick left behind. Many taste like fruits or honey and are completely lickable.
Sprinkle it on: Kama Sutra Honey Dust, Love Dust.

Make your own honey dust. Mix one tablespoon of vanilla powder with one cup of corn starch or cornflour. Work in one tablespoon of pure honey, rubbing the clumps between your fingers until they turn into very tiny particles. Apply and lick off.

Don't limit yourself to just body paints. Chocolate, sundae toppings, jams – you can use any foodstuff.

When you want to make it wetter: If sex has turned into a dry affair lately, you need to add a lube to the mix (see Chapter 3, p.39, for the basics).
Squeeze it on: Astroglide, ID Glide.

When you want to custom design it: Create a masterpiece on the naked canvas with body paints in vivid colours. Although flavoured, many are actually too bitter to really get any licking-off pleasure from (with the exception of chocolate paint). And they have incredible staying power so leave some time for showering off afterward. While the paint isn't particularly great for finger work, it comes with a small brush that could be sold as a sex toy in its own right.
Dab it on: Body Paints, Body Frosting, Kama Sutra Lover's Paintbox, Tom and Sally's Chocolate Body Paint, Body Talk Chocolate Tattoo Kit, Glow In The Dark Body Paints (not edible).

While playing "X Marks the Spot" seems obvious, it's actually hotter to skip the dot, dot, dot moves and use long strokes running the length of the body.

When you want to light a fire: Take the S&M out of melted wax with a candle that doubles up as scented massage oil. While the wax can be used cold, why would you when it's so much fun to light the candle, drip the wax on and rub it in? (See the candle safety tipbit on p.115.)
Melt it: Lava Lotion

> *If the ointment is mint-flavoured, stick with a sheer coat as it can have a numbing action when slathered on – not the effect you are after.*

When you want to make sex sweeter: Feasting on edible oils and gels from each other's bodies will satisfy any cravings you have for desert – and they're calorie free. However, they may be messy, they may be sticky and they may give you toothache.
Season it: ID Juicy Lubes, Wet Fun Flavours Oils, Hot Licks, Good Head Gel, Shunga Aphrodisiac Oil, Nipple Drops.

> *Some oils heat up when used, to keep things cooking. Hot breath works better than cold to keep them sizzling.*

When you don't want any mess: Flavoured foam in a can – what could be better for the clean-and-tidy type who wants to make things squishy and fun but can't let go of what the oils and creams and dust and things might do to the duvet? The foam, which looks a lot like hair mousse, sits exactly where you put it, no running or dripping, until it's licked off.
Smarten it up: Eros Fun Foam.

When you want to make it last: These potions are for overly anxious men, giving them the control they need to prolong your pleasure. There's no secret magic ingredient – most contain the numbing chemical benzocaine or some natural alternative ingredient. Think carefully before applying as he may end up staying in the action long after either of you have any interest.
Firm it up: Power Delay Sta-Erect Not Yet Delay Gel-O, Durex Maintain Desensitizing Lubricant for Men Double Pack, Staying Power.

> *Delaying lotion needs to be applied to the head and shaft of the penis about ten minutes before intercourse in order to take effect when you need it to. It must be washed off afterwards.*

98

5 last answers to those questions you have about lotions and potions but are afraid to ask

My boyfriend gave me what he thought would be a sexy massage but the oil he used burned me.
He used a cheap brand – and therefore, cheap ingredients – or he used a handyman's special and had a heavy hand when adding the scent – you only need a few drops of essential oil per palmful of oil. Add more and it can feel like you have fire ants crawling on your body – instead of sex, all you'll want is to jump into an ice cold pool.

Grease slicks can be removed with any commercial oil-stain remover.

Never use undiluted essential oil on the skin.

Whenever my husband gives me a massage he stops after fifteen minutes, saying his hands are tired.
First of all, send the boy to a gym to build up his stamina. In the meantime, pick up a tool made specifically for massage. Happy Heart is a manual massager uniquely angled to fit the curves of your body (including your lurve lines) while PureBliss, Rubba Ducky, Hitachi Magic Wand and Fukuoku Glove are vibrators that will ease his work load and pile on the relaxing vibes for you.

We were fooling around with body paints and now my sheets have big stains.
Wash and wash again. While many body paints are water soluble, some are not so easy to get out of your linens. If the paints don't come out after a few washings, you may have to toss them out. Next time, keep the 200+ thread count and satin sheets for when you are just planning to cuddle up.

Body dusts can make a mess that takes weeks to clean up. But most also come with a feather tickler of some sort. If yours didn't, pick one up. Not only will the feeling of the feather tickling the skin add a new sensuous twist to your love games, it will also keep the dust from clumping or getting all over the room.

Chocolate is hard to wash off your body – you sometimes need a few showers even after your lover has feasted his fill. So don't have a sexy choc-fest unless you have time for grooming after.

Are oils condom-safe?
It depends on the oil – you will need to read the label or ask the manufacturer. Note: any lotion or potion containing oil can destroy your latex contraception (that includes diaphragms and caps) within 60 seconds. It doesn't matter what kind of oil. Note this too: chocolate contains oil. Now go back to Chapter 3 to see what else you need to stay clear of.

What are the sexiest scents?
According to essential-oil makers, ylang-ylang, patchouli and jasmine work like a poor-man's Viagra. Steer clear of lavender as it puts you to sleep. Stimulating oils (hitting all body parts) include neroli and rosemary. Sniff away.

Rub down

There's nothing that says, "I adore you and want to bang you into the next calendar year", quite like a deep, penetrating massage. To prepare for your night of rubdown heaven, you'll need a few mood setters as well as techniques. Crack your knuckles and prepare your fingers for their venture on to (and in to) each other's bodies.

Oil-based lube and massage oils are not great for slathering the vagina because the oil doesn't wash out easily, which can make it a bacteria nursery. Nor are they latex-safe if that's your contraceptive material of choice (see Chapter 3, p.37).

Despite what you might think, a lighter oil is better. Since you'll be varnishing it all over your bodies, the last thing you want is a sticky coat you can scrape off with your nails. Lighter oils also have lighter scents, which means neither of you will keel over from the overwhelming perfumes found in some oils (especially the warming oils).

What you "knead"
You'll need:

Massage oil: A well-lubed massage feels much better than a dry one. You can get everything from scented and edible oils to oils that heat up either with the touch of a hand or someone blowing on it (see Lotions and Potions, p.98). There's a good reason some are more expensive than others – they don't absorb into the skin too quickly so they last longer while you're softly kneading away. Work it with: Kama Sutra Massage Oils (good for the whole body), Wet Platinum Lubricant (best on genitals), Wet Lite Lubricant (best on genitals), ID Glide Sensual Lubricant (best on genitals).

Pleasure mitt, vibrating fingers or massage wand
See Chapters 5 and 8 for caressing, massaging, and tantalizing.

Scented candles to set the mood

How to get touchy-feely
There is really no set sequence to giving a massage. Generally, it's best to just go with the flow and concentrate on areas with a lot of tension in them or purposely build the tension in your partner's favourite hot spots. However, if you're the rule-following sort who must have a specific order to follow, try the following first, then mix it up to keep your partner on edge:

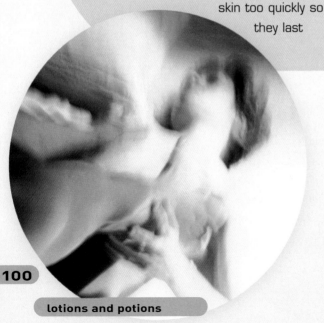

Stroke it

Massage is basically a series of strokes – the main thing is to keep a slow, gentle steady rhythm and use a little bit of pressure (translation: tease, don't squeeze). Repeat each move at least three times before starting a new stroke.

Here are the basics – mix and match as you see fit. Go barehanded or use a vibrating toy for all or part of the play (see Chapter 5):

♥ Rub in circles.

♥ Use the entire hand as much as possible – the palm and the fingers pressed-together.

♥ Knead with your fingers.

♥ Pound gently with the sides of your hands.

♥ Slide your hands along the length of the body.

♥ Lean into your stroke when you want to increase the pressure.

♥ Brush the skin with fingertips.

♥ Tug on pubic hair.

♥ Let other parts of your body rub up against his body while in the midst of your massage.

♥ After you do anything that may be a little on the rougher side, do something light, smooth and soft.

♥Neck and shoulders to relieve any tension

♥ Back, sides and buttocks

♥ Legs

♥ Head and face will bring you closer, before you start on more intimate regions

♥ Breasts/nipples

♥ Belly

♥ Genitals

Massage the other bits for at least 30 minutes before moving on to #s 5 or 7.

You'd think the bed was the best place for a massage. Think again. It's too soft, putting to much strain on the receiver. Instead, pad the floor with some blankets or lie on a thick carpet.

It's best to get undressed first so you don't worry about getting an oil stain on your favourite dress. And it sets the mood right away.

That is, as long as you've cranked up the heat – bring it to 70°F (21°C) and stay out of draughts.

It's always good to keep your massage oil warm. Cold oil and hands can not only kill the mood, but also make him shrivel faster than an electric saw heading towards his private parts. Just dunk the bottle of oil in a bowl of hot tap water. And rub the oil into your hands, so they stay warm too.

CHAPTER 10
bottoms up

The person on the anal receiving end is usually referred to as the "bottom", and the partner doing the penetrating, is called the "top".

Either you are going to read this chapter because you've:
a) tried **BOOTY BUMPING** and **love it**;
b) are CURIOUS about giving booty bumping a go;
c) never ever want to try it but you want to know what the **hooplah** is.

Everyone else is going to skip ahead to the next chapter. Which is a shame, because the fact is that the bottom has more nerve endings than any other part of your body save the genitals. Touching, licking, and massaging it alone can feel exquisite. From the entry (AKA the anus) to the two sphincter muscles that make up its canal and elastic folds of tissue that wrap lovingly around anything in their path to the actual rectum, it is the road to pure bliss when stimulated. In men, the rectum is actually the gateway to prostate massage, which can trigger a put-his-balls-in-a-knot orgasm. Plus it's an accommodating host, stretching to receive whatever comes in (or out).

Most people's main concern with anal sex is, quite rightly, pain. But the truth is, anal sex performed the correct way is pleasurable, not painful. You really are better off sticking a toy as opposed to his penis or fingers up there. Here's why: the tissues and membranes in the anus are ultra-thin, making them extremely delicate. So being creative and sticking just anything in your rectum can be dodgy. Some items can be sucked into the rectum. And you can't just push them out with your next bowel movement. Most of the time, it's a very embarrassing, very painful trip to hospital to have the object removed via a proctoscope – which is about as fun as it sounds. Anal toys, on the other hand, are made of smooth materials so the anal membranes don't get scraped or ripped. And they are made with a flared base or extra-long bases to ensure they do not travel too far into the rectum past the point of no return.

Another hesitation regarding anal sex is that it seems dirty to stick things up the same place that bowel movements come out of. Using a toy lets you experiment if you're fastidious about getting your hands (or other parts) dirty.

Anal sex is not abnormal unless you think it is. Sex is all about adults playing with each other making each other feel good. As long as you're both agreeing to the activities, there's nothing unnatural about it.

RULES OF ENGAGEMENT

Anal sex does not have to hurt. When you stick something up your bum, your internal sphincters involuntarily tense up. The way to get around this is to relax. Here's your ten-step plan to getting in a mellow frame of mind before bottom dipping:

1 Get a manicure. You need to trim those nails – even if you don't plan to stick your fingers in. Unless you plan to insert the toy with your teeth (and that's a whole new sharp issue), your hands will still be holding the toy which means they will be working around the bottom and need to be smooth.

Skip any lubes with nonoxynol-9 – it's a detergent and irritating to delicate anal tissue.

2 Take a bath. For one thing, it will relax you. And for another, it will wash out your bottom so everything is squeaky clean.

3 Don't forget the power of foreplay before, during and after and all night long if desired.

4 Use lube. Grease your bottom hole, your toy of choice, and the fingers that are doing the installation. After you think you've put on enough, add some more. The rectum is not self-lubricating like the vagina and penis. Plus, it is made to be an exit, not an entrance.

Desensitizers contain a mild anaesthetic (7.5 per cent benzocaine), which causes a temporary numbing sensation after being applied to the skin. The problem is that the gel or cream can rub off onto the other partner's genitals or mouth, making your love-meld feel like a trip to the dentist.

The best lubes for anal play:
• Thicker, creamier, and water-based will really stay on the job: Slippery Stuff Gel.
• Second-string favourites: ID Glide, Maximus, Liquid Silk.
• If you want to numb things with a light desensitizer for easier entry and aren't using latex contraception: Anal Eze.

5 Get in position. Top three moves are:

• On your back, with a pillow under your butt.
• On your back with your legs up in the air.
• On your knees, doggie style (you will need to tighten your bottom muscles a bit which will be easier if you have some support under your chest/belly to lean on. If you lean forward a little, extending your legs out and to the side behind you, this should put things at an easier angle for access).

The person on the receiving end can push down slightly with their bottom muscles (as if making a bowel movement) to relax the sphincter.

If you've lubed up as much as you should have, then the person who is in charge of penetration action is going to have to wipe their fingers before moving the toy in and out or permanently out or else their digits will be too slippery to get a good grip.

It helps if you play with your lover's other hot zones as you slide the toy in to keep things sizzling. Oral sex is especially body melting at this moment.

If it hurts, stop but don't remove for about a minute. The pain will subside as the muscle gets used to the feeling and begins to relax.

6 Like any good workout, you need to warm up first with a little finger rubbing – gently massage the anus with two fingers in light circular strokes (you can wear a latex glove for this). As your partner relaxes, you should be able to slip in a finger or two (do it with the pads of your finger first as they are much gentler than the tips). Make sure you finger is slightly curved toward the front of the body to work in the direction of the passage. Don't automatically thrust your finger in and out. Once it penetrates, hold it still until you feel the muscles relax.

7 Check in with each other regularly. Don't just assume there's no pain – ask and, if asked, answer truthfully. If it hurts, it will hurt more if you keep on doing it. Instead, go back to Step #3.

8 Get ready to slide your toy in. Slowly and gently. Keep up with Step #7. Remember, you're both playing together, you're not just ramming stuff in your lover's

If your toy is tough to clean, you can skip the scrub down if you slip a condom over it before inserting it. But if you're planning on an all-day plug up, change the condom throughout the day — they're tough, but they're not made to last for hours of use.

bottom. The best method is probably to make a slight pumping motion, starting out just pushing slightly at the opening, not actually penetrating at all, and simply adding the tiniest bit of pressure each time. It should literally take you minutes to make any real progress.

9 When finished, hold the base of your toy and slowly pull out. Too fast a tug can cause your partner's sphincter muscles to cramp.

10 Clean everything up (see Chapter 4).

Never switch your anal toy to your vagina without a thorough clean.

Tools of the trade

ANAL BEADS (AKA love beads, bum/butt beads or string of pearls): They may be shiny and come in a rainbow of colours, but these jewels are worn where the sun don't shine. Great for up the butt beginners, beads seem to have a classier kudos than other anal toys – think of it as adorning your bottom. The beads are usually made up of around six small balls connected with a piece of nylon cord and a pull ring for extraction. Ball size varies from a small bead to as large as a golf ball. Beginners should obviously start small, but not too small, as the beads have to be large enough to make an impression – 1cm (1/2 inch) is a good launcher. You can also work your way up to a longer string of beads.

The balls may also be connected by a flexible rod, or stacked in a row like a beaded wand – abracadabra. This makes them easier to clean, insert and remove. Also, depending on their stiffness and length, they may penetrate deeper. Some beads also vibrate.

Although they are available in every kind of material (see Chapter 1, pp.22-5), silicone is the best for beads as it can be boiled (an important point when you think where they're going). If you can only spring for plastic, you're probably going to have to smooth down the rough seams with a nail file before using (or you could learn a painful lesson). They are difficult to clean and the string part can get nasty, especially at the knots and where it meets the bead, where "stuff" can get trapped.

The bottom line: Insert into the bottom slowly, one bead at a time, in single file; leaving the ring outside. After all, you need something to pull them out with (if your set doesn't have a handle or ring on the end, be sure to leave at least one bead outside to grip for removal). The hole will close around and "swallow" each bead. If using string type beads, you can push them in further with your finger or just let the next bead inserted push the string higher. Some people like them pulled out all at once during orgasm to pile on the pleasure. Others prefer them to be removed one-by-one just before or after orgasm. When the time comes, grip the handle or end of the beads and pull firmly and

steadily (don't yank on them). Keep pulling as the beads come out one by one. The orgasmic contractions of the rectum should help to force them out. As the beads exit the rectum, the anal sphincter is forced open and shut again and again. These extra waves of stimulation can take you from cloud 9 to cloud 99.

BUTT PLUGS: A butt plug is a kind of bowling pin-shaped mini dildo. But instead of using it to go in and out, you use it to go in and stay in. The shape and flared base means it only goes so deep and will sit in the butt and not come out until you're ready. You can use it any time – some people wear them all day. You can go from small training plugs the size of your small finger to extra large fist-sized ones. There are inflatable plugs which mean you can go from small to large without buying four different plugs. Some also vibrate – which is great for beginners to loosen up and relax bottom-wise. Other plugs have ridges to add some extra friction as they go in.

The bottom line: Lube it up and angle it up toward the front of the body. Go slowly (if it's ribbed, push in one rib at a time, holding still after each rib goes in). If you're feeling daring, try twisting the

The smaller butt plugs don't always stay in as well as larger ones, because their base is almost as wide as the largest part of the narrowed section.

Fill yourself up with a silicone butt plug and then touch the base with a vibrator and blast off. Silicone transmits vibration better than any other material.

Some dildos are tipped to tickle his prostate.

plug slightly in order to the insert the thickest part. Do the same backwards to remove it.

DILDOS: Using a dildo gives you more control over the amount of pressure hitting the anus during insertion, and greater control over your own movements. There are dildos made specifically for the bottom, dildos manufactured to ring your front or rear doorbell and double-headed dildos that play both ends of your field at the same time (see Chapter 6, p.71). Don't use a dildo that does not make of point of mentioning that it is bottom friendly.

The bottom line: Start by slowly stretching your bottom hold with fingers and even a butt plug first. Then smear everything with plenty of lube and slowly insert the dildo. Because a dildo doesn't have a small tip, you will need to just get used to the dilation at first. Hold still, then thrust slowly and check in with your partner to see what they want it deeper, harder, slower or faster. Never assume, "Okay it's in, so I can thrust vigorously." You may never get to that point.

See the vibrator tipbit under butt plugs (p.106).

TOP PLAYERS

They may not be the prettiest toys on the shelf, but these are the ones that get the job done:

TOY TYPE	FOR NEWBIES	FOR OLD-HANDS
Prostate Stimulation	Aneros	Aneros
Butt Plugs	The Essential Plug	The Ripple
Beads	Kama Sutra Graduated Beads	Power Balls
Dildo	Blue Silk	Dangerous Curves
Vibrator	The Enticer	Tail Spin

Everything you need to ease in
Beginner's Anal Pleasure Kit, Ultra 4 Professional Anal Kit

ANAL VIBES: These are like anorexic vaginal vibes. The buzzing helps relax the sphincter muscles so it's easier to slide in. Some come with extra doodas to rub other bits of your body at the same time.

The bottom line: Insertion is pretty much the same as for a dildo. Start your engines before going in so it's vibrating all the way to the bull's eye. Once in, move it in, move it out, shake it all about for a full bottom massage.

5 last answers to those questions you have about going in backward but are afraid to ask

I want to use anal toys but I'm scared it's going to be dirty and smelly.

Your bottom-hole is not a holding cell for your crap. That's the colon's job and your toy is not going to come anywhere near that port of call. It is a good idea, however, to try and take a loo break and hit the shower to scrub down with soap first. Some people like to do an enema to houseclean before knocking on the back door, but that's not really necessary and can be dangerous if done too often

No matter how well you clean, there are always trace elements left – not enough to see or feel or become disgusted by, but enough to cause infection if not washed properly. So it is critical to scrub anything that has come in contact with the anus, especially before moving on to other kinds of sex.

I tried to use anal beads but couldn't get the things up my butt.

You think you have a freakishly small/sensitive anal opening? It's unlikely. The rectum is actually quite big. Fact is, most people don't get to actual penetration the first time they try anal toys. Think of it as learning to ride a bike – it takes a while to get the balance right. And remember – you can never have too much lube or foreplay.

108

Could a dildo get stuck up you permanently? We used one for the first time and it felt like that was about to happen so I made my boyfriend take it out.

Only if you use a toy that is not made for anal play and then stick it in too deep. If you did and didn't, then it sounds like you just needed to go slower. It sounds like your sphincter muscles aren't relaxed enough to accommodate whatever is going in it. With more of a warm up, you'll be more aroused and it should feel much better.

I just started using anal toys and love them! The only thing is, after a long session my bottom is so sore I can't sit down the next day.

Take a break for a few days. When you are ready to start playing again, stock up on haemorrhoidal wipes – pre-moistened wipes with witch hazel and aloe. They'll immediately calm an itchy, sore, or irritated butt.

If your partner squeals in pain and screams "STOP!" then do so immediately.

How long is too long for wearing a butt plug?

It mainly depends on how long you can go without taking a dump. If you are trying to break world records, then plug up right after you go and eat as little as possible while wearing your bottom accessory.

You should be an experienced anal player before trying this. Begin by wearing a butt plug for a half hour, see how it feels, how you like it, what works and what doesn't. If your thirty-minute excursion goes well, try an hour next time. Continue building up (in reasonable increments) the amount of time that you wear the plug.

You may want to consider taking the butt plug out every hour, re-lubing it and re-inserting it. Otherwise, the lube ends up being absorbed by your body, making the plug feel uncomfortable.

For those who never forgot their Scouts training and like to prepare for every eventuality, take a few precautions to make sure your plug doesn't pop out at an inopportune moment — like when meeting your in-laws. Wear a butt-plug harness (very similar to a dildo harness — see Chapter 6, p.73). A very tight pair of underwear, briefs, or a thong will also do the trick, depending on the size of the plug and how strong those sphincter muscles are.

part **four**

fun & games

This next section is for the sexually adventurous.

Wait! Don't close the book before you've read this newsflash: getting into a little bondage lite and dressing up in mistress or master clothing does not automatically qualify you for official membership to the sicko club. The sexually uninhibited are not a bunch of panting nymphos scrounging for their next hump-mate. Rather they (hopefully that means you) are voracious connoisseurs, forever searching for new experiences – sexual and otherwise. People who are willing to at least take a quick stroll on the wild side love to play and have lots of imagination when it comes to figuring out how to make things fun and sensuous. In fact, research shows that your tendency to seek out new experiences says a lot about your lust level. The more open you are to trying new things, the higher your overall gratification.

Even if you don't think bondage is something you want to make a part of your erotic life, these toys are worth checking out if you are on the hunt for ways to climb out of a sexual rut with your partner – you can act out fantasies, play games for high orgasmic stakes, find a fun gift for your next lover's day or just have a laugh.

CHAPTER 11
whips, chains and orgies, oh my!

It seems a real stretch of the imagination to consider that even the potential of **PAIN** is sexy. But here are seven ways in which getting **TIED UP**, **spanked**, **gagged**, **DOMINATED** or playing the **dominatrix** can make your sex life **SIZZLE**:

1 It may just make you want to get married: letting someone tie you up requires a great deal of trust and intimacy – so does committing yourself to someone.

2 It's a powerful turn on to be either a) completely helpless and have someone you know have their wicked way with you; or b) the person having their wicked way.

3 Finally, all the anxiety is taken out of lovemaking – after all, you're either tied up so what can you do; or you are doing exactly what you want to do it how you want it done – what could be better?

4 It can be an erotic trip during which every sense is awakened.

5 You burn more calories. When your body is challenged in any way, everything starts working harder, giving you the equivalent of a cardio workout.

6 It makes you high. When spanked, the brain kicks in with endorphins, natural chemicals that produce a "runner's high", to balance out the pain.

7 You'll never be lonely. Kinsey reported that about half of all men and women are aroused by being bitten. Other studies have found that around one-third of all couples have tried spanking at least once and about as many have engaged in mild bondage by tying up a sexual partner. Countless others include horseplay in their lovemaking – slapping, light spanking, teasing, tickling mercilessly and pinching.

Ready to submit yet?
No experience necessary.

Know the code

In almost any kind of kinky sex it is essential to make a code word between you; some version of 'stop', in case what is being done does not feel good to the person it is being done to or they need a bathroom break or they've had enough. Sometimes in the throes of passion people say things like "oh no" or "oh stop, stop!" when role-playing, so make it a word or phrase you usually wouldn't say during sex, such as, "Rolf Harrison". It is essential that when the code word is used, all action stops immediately.

Play it out

When most people think of bondage they think of a person being tied up and beaten. But bondage doesn't have to be about pain.
Try these different bondage levels on for size (you'll need to decide who is going to be restrained and who is going to be free – or take turns):

Take the guesswork out of your shopping list:
♥ *The Romantic Restraint Kit has everything you need for entry-level bondage: velcro cuffs, leather blindfold and a tickler.*
♥ *The Beginners B&D Kit ups the power play with an instructional video, a sturdy set of leather wrist restraints, a latex whip, leather paddle, collar, two tie-off straps or leash, and a comfortable blindfold.*

Level one: Restraint only
No spanking, whipping, paddling or flogging is involved. One of you is tied up and ravished.
You'll need: restraints*

Level two: Lover's talk
One of you is still tied up but this time the one in control teases the other by describing everything they are going to do before they do it – think of it as verbal foreplay.
You'll need: restraints*

Level three: Tease it
The person tied up is tormented and teased with different types of stimulation. If you want to add an explosive power play to the mix, the one dominating tells the other they can't orgasm until given permission. Two tricks to try:

1 Have him tie you up so you are spread-eagled to the bed with a turned-on vibrator between your legs so it's just hitting your love button. While he plays with your breasts alternating between using an ice cube and a fur-covered mitt, you'll be writhing your hips around, trying to get the vibrator to touch exactly where and when you want it.

2 Taunt the restrained person with feathers. Try the Feather Pleasure, a synthetic (so no chance of allergies!) ostrich feather with a bamboo wand.
You'll need: whatever toys strike your fancy, restraints*.

Level four: lose your senses
Sex is all about senses – putting yours in someone else's control is hot, hot, hot:

1 **Sight:** put on a blindfold and your sense of touch becomes intense. Plus, you drool with anticipation because you don't know when and where you'll next be touched.

2 **Touch:** obviously, you can't really make a person's sense of touch go away completely, but you can make it more sensitive:
♥ Alternate hot and cold by running ice over their body and then dripping hot wax on them (see safety tip at top of p.115).

114

Use a paraffin candle — they burn at a lower temperature and cool off more quickly than regular candles. When dripping candle wax, make sure you start by holding the candle high up away from the body, so it cools a little before it hits the skin.

♥ Intensify pinches with nipple or clitoral clamps.

Don't put clamps on your lover until they are turned-on and always apply to the tip — not the whole nipple or clitoris. Remove after 30 minutes.

3 Sound: you can use sound to add to the tension or create a relaxed mood. Headphones make it possible for your lover to hear certain types of music or sounds (nature CDs, people making love CDs, erotic story CDs, etc.) or just the sound of your voice.

4 Taste: re-enact the famous scene from 9½ Weeks – rent it for a pre-play turn on.

If you want to block out sound, use earmuffs.

5 Smell: check out Chapter 9 for different scented lotions.

Level five: Learn your role

When you role-play, the sense of drama is all in the action. See Acting Out, p.120, for power play ideas.

Level six: Hit me with your rhythm stick

Surprise: spanking does not have to involve pain – unless you both want it to. Here's how to keep it safe:

♥ Mainly spank the bottom (be sure to keep away from the kidneys and the spine!). This will stimulate the nerves and sends blood rushing to the entire pelvic region. Never ever strike: directly on a bone (spine, collar bone, elbows, knee caps and shins), the neck or head, the lower back (the kidneys are located just under the skin), or the back of the knees.

♥ Proceed with caution: don't give it your all from the first hit. Start off striking lightly, then gradually make the strikes more intense. Rub your lover's skin that has just been smacked with your hand or other soft object. Remember, this is a sensuous erotic event, not a beating.

♥ Gently drag the flogger over the skin, letting the person get a feel for the instrument and get excited about what's coming.

♥ The shorter the flogger, the more control you have over where it lands. The shortest ones can be great for intense genital play or any time you want precision. The longer, heavier ones are going to have more of an impact when they land (in other words, they have more of a thud feeling). General rule of thumb: for optimal control, a flogger should be about as long as the distance between your nose and your bellybutton (including the tail and the handle).

♥ The more tails in a flogger, the more of a thud you're going to encounter. The width of the tails can make a difference as well; very thin tails will be more whippy and stingy (like a cat o' nine tails or a bullwhip – for serious sting aficionados) whereas very wide tails will feel heavier and deliver more of a "slap" feeling.

♥ The softest floggers are made out of velvety deerskin and feel like a deeply satisfying, relaxing rub down when used, bringing your blood slowly to the surface of your skin for a warm feeling.

♥ There are many whips available that don't hurt at all, no matter how hard they're swung. Some – like the Latex Whip on a Stick – even sound painful when they come into contact with the skin, but are more likely to make you giggle than say ouch.

♥ Rubber is intensely stingy – it is possible to draw blood with it.

♥ Paddles deliver a more concentrated impact because they're usually wide and flat. Some paddles are made with soft cushy material on one side for a playful cushy smack, but the other side is usually leather for that more intense smack so you can rotate between soft and hard. But most are made of leather and deliver an impact similar to that of a ruler.

Three Must-Follow Rules (read before you strike)

1 When spanking your lover, there are some parts of the body you should never spank, no matter what tool you use. Hands off:

• directly hitting the spine, collar bone, elbows, kneecaps, and shins. Being hit on a bone area feels about as sexy as breaking your toe.

Once the person who is tied up does their bliss shake, release them. The party's over.

• The neck or head (you may knock the person unconscious).

• The lower back (the kidneys are located just under the skin).

2 Practice makes perfect: work with your tool before using it on your lover so that you don't accidentally hit a sensitive part of your lover's body. Whips especially are easy to lose control of.

3 Always rest after spanking. Allow the sensation to register in your lover's mind and on his/her skin.

Off-the-shelf S&M

Bondage toys are designed to provide their unique type of pleasure safely. They release quickly, are padded for your comfort and are made of materials your skin loves. That said, there are plenty of ways to explore your dark side without much financial layout:

♥ Don't be an accessories hound. You can have kinky sex with no equipment at all: all it takes is a little gentle scratching, pinching, light bites and soft spanking to intensify the fun.

♥ Lots of inexpensive props work just as well as pricey restraints: try thick yarn, scarves, nylons or rope (keep scissors handy to snip the knots rather than trying to undo them once you're finished).

♥ Buy leashes and dog collars in pet shops.

♥ Get an eye mask from any beauty supply store.

♥ Use a household ruler or flat-headed hairbrush for a paddle.

Fasten your safety belts

Two rules to memorize before you get all tied up.

♥ Choose your material carefully. Restraints can easily damage the skin and may cause long-term damage to tendons and joints if worn too long or incorrectly. Even soft material like silk scarves, bandannas and nylons (which have a nasty habit of tightening under tension) sometimes get so tight they have to be cut off. And handcuffs made of metal can cause lead to nerve and bone damage, sometime irreparably – not the sexy outcome you were hoping for.

Even purchased restraints are not one-need-fits-all. See below to see which match your desire:

♥ You want to break out quickly: nylon webbing ankle and wrist cuffs that fasten with Velcro will give you a secure fit that is easy to get out of in a pinch.

Best buy: Jane's Bonds (a big plus – they come with handy 120cm (4 ft) tethers attached so you can tie someone up just about anywhere), Tease-Me Cuffs, Sports Cuffs.

♥ You want to be trussed up: the shape and super-strength of D or O-rings means you can clip someone's wrists or ankles together, or if you want to clip them to something, you can attach connectors.

Best buy: Kookie cuffs, Joshua Tree cuffs.

You want it to be simple but still look like BDSM gear: Go for buckles which are a snap to adjust but have the right look and come in leather as well.

Best buy: Fleece-lined Leather Handcuffs

You want to play lock-up: handcuffs are usually first choice for bondage first-timers, but they're actually accidents waiting to happen. Most cheap handcuffs lock in place with levers – which can be moved and tightened up during play (FYI: not a good thing). Fur makes the cuffs more comfy and cool than cold, hard metal. Plus you can colour coordinate them to your outfit.

Best buy: Furry Cuffs, Deluxe Locking Cuffs (not for amateurs).

You want comfort with your bondage: the most comfortable cuffs out there are leather. They're padded, very cushy, wide and usually fasten with buckles. They're also usually expensive, so if you're just starting, leather should be your next step.

Best buy: Leather Love Wear Leather Handcuffs (less pricey but no extra padding), Lavender Wrist and Ankle Cuffs.

You name it, you can be restrained in it — there are bondage chairs, sofas, beds and counters.

You want to turn your bed into a low security gaol: Sports Sheets are actually a mattress sheet and four nylon cuffs for wrists and ankles that Velcro to the sheets for some quick spread-eagled fun. A dream for beginners, the restrained partner can very easily break free by lifting their limbs. Adaptable for all mattress sizes.

The in-case-you-run-out-of-packing-tape toy: bondage tape sticks to itself only — not skin or hair. It's heavy duty, yet you can cut someone free with a simple pair of surgical scissors. It's available in a 20m (65ft) roll.

Read this before going under lock-down:

♥ Make sure the cuffs aren't too tight (your wrist should be able to move around).

♥ Don't create tension (other than the sexual kind) – arms should feel comfortable, not pulled apart.

♥ Don't put any weight on the cuffs (as in lying on your back with your handcuffed hands under you).

♥ Ignore the phone if you have a cuffed lover in your bedroom. What if the house is catches on fire? There's an earthquake? Any sort of emergency? A helpless person is just that: helpless.

♥ Take your time restraining your lover. Doing it slowly makes the experience more erotic. Plus you can make sure you get it right.

♥ Anything that puts any pressure AT ALL on the front of the neck can lead to unconsciousness quickly, as the carotid arteries go right to the brain. Likewise be careful with gags or things tied in the mouth; as well as restricting breathing, they can trigger a gag reflex, which could be really nasty if the person who is tied up can't get the gag out.

♥ Their limbs will "fall asleep" if they can't move them. Pins and needles are not lite pain fun.

♥ Always keep scissors handy just in case.

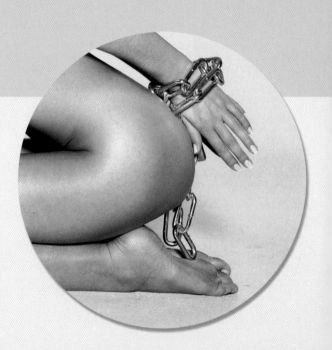

118

5 last answers to those questions you have about bondage but are afraid to ask

I used rope to tie him up and then I couldn't undo the knot.
This is why bondage sex toys were invented. Still, it always helps to have at least one good knot under your belt – here is a common slip knot which is sturdy but easy to undo:
1. Take a piece of rope. Call one end A, and the other B.
2. Make a loop (1) near the A end so that B lies over and not under at the cross.
3. Holding the loop together, make another loop (2) at the B end.
4. Push (2) loop through (1) loop.
5. Pull at A end and (2) loop to tighten.

The key broke in the handcuffs.
Get a metal file and start filing. If you want to play with handcuffs, get a good-quality pair with a double lock so you can snap them on and then lock them so they won't get tighter under pressure (as cheap cuffs will) and a pin-point that fits in a hole after the cuffs have been put on to secure the size.
Best buy: Peerless Cuffs.

We had a safe word but then he gagged me as part of the game and couldn't understand when I said "porcupine".
Next time, hold a white hanky or bright coloured scarf – if you let go, that's your SOS signal.

We tried playing doctor and nurse and felt silly.
So try again. The basic idea with all this is to experiment. The first few times you won't really know what you're doing so chances are it's not going to work wonderfully. Take your time trying different games, different positions, different costumes, whatever. There's a lot of kink to choose from – eventually you'll hit on a favourite.

He likes whips and chains, but I'm more of a satin sheets girl.
If your fantasies clash, you might find yourself at the far end of the bed – or worse, completely grossed out. While you obviously can't do something that makes you feel uncomfortable, you can compromise – for instance, if your wildest sex involves acting out a steamy love scene as a saucy French maid and master while he's more of the leather school, maybe he can speak French to you and you can wear a leather skirt during sex. Most important is to be true to yourself and what you want. Never compromise your own feelings and boundaries for the sake of maintaining a relationship. Only you can decide what you can live – and sleep – with ... and without.

Sometimes it helps to start your big acting scene after the sex action has begun because it makes you feel less self-conscious.

Avoid cuffs with cloverleaf keys as the motion of your lovemaking can cause the cheap sliding lever of the double lock mechanism to slip and the cuffs to release (ruining your fun) or tighten (ruining your fun).

119

Acting out

You don't need professional sets or best-selling plots to get into character. Do sexual improv. Yes, it will definitely feel a bit ridiculous at first pretending you're a maiden captured by a lusty pirate, but all this acting out can make the other power-play stuff feel more comfortable – that's not your sweet lover-boy handcuffing you to the bed, it's the intruder who has broken into your bedroom to rape you (yes, these fantasies are okay – it's about surrendering control, not really wanting the thing to happen).

Putting on a costume just makes it easier to get the scene moving along. Plus, it's just plain fun – think about going to a fancy dress party. The best part is dressing up as something you're not. Sometimes, just the feel of a material you wouldn't normally be caught dead in is enough to get you off.

Yes, this all requires a tremendous amount of imagination on your part. But so does believing the plot lines of the daytime soaps – you can do it!

Calling wardrobe!

What exactly is sexy clothing? Well, it depends who you ask. Silky lingerie, fishnets and safety pins, riding clothes, a tweed skirt and pressed white blouse; guaranteed, someone, somewhere, is going to get off on it.

Which means you can basically put together a dressing up box by scouring your local charity shop. Or log on to your favourite sex boutique. Here are the top best-selling looks you won't see on the high street this year:

Wench outfit: all you need is a medieval lager lout and a roaring fire.

Sexy nurse uniform: watch his temperature heat up.

Fireman's uniform: baby, he can put out your fire anytime.

Sexy school girl outfit: think of the fun assignments he can give you.

Pirate's outfit: Yo ho ho!

French maid costume: Oohlala!

Military uniform: drop and do ten push-ups in the buff.

Fishnet cat suit: Meow!

Baby doll lingerie: You won't catch any zzz's in this.

Leather clothing (bustier, thong, corset): just add studs.

Latex clothing (bustier, bodysuit, corset, thong): you'll feel shiny and smooth.

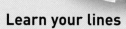

Sometimes, all you need to do is slip on a simple mask to give your play a sexy anonymous feel.

The unforgiving nature of fabric like latex or leather means that getting dressed requires a certain degree of pre-prep – powder or lube your body before climbing in. Go for a non-greasy solution like Eros (it'll also make your body feel super silky). Also, these materials don't breathe well so pile on the deodorant – you will sweat.

If your role-playing doesn't feel right, try switching roles. You may feel more comfortable in dominant (person calling the shots) mode, while he may enjoy being the submissive (person doing what they're told), or vice versa.

Learn your lines

When you're coming up with a scene, keep it simple at first. Avoid characters and plot-lines that are complicated, or you'll lose your steam trying to work them out. Once you have your stage legs, you can push the roles even further and even cross the lines of reality: for example, use a real camera to make the porn fantasy authentic.

Here are a few scenes to get warmed up with – these can go on for as long days or last as long as Britney Spears' Las Vegas marriage.

If a little bondage is part of your scene, make sure you pre-agree on how far the pain can go – say only mild spanking and/or verbal humiliation.

SLAVE/MASTER: The slave has stolen something from the master and now must be punished.

STRIPPER/CUSTOMER: One of you is the exotic dancer, the other is the spectator. Follow the rules: tip generously, and while the dancer can touch the spectator, he/she can't touch the dancer.

"ESCORT"/CLIENT: One of you plays a rich client a high-class escort for the evening. The client leaves money on the dresser, and lets the escort do all the work (make polite conversation for a minute or so, and then gets down to business, saying all the things you normally wouldn't).

PORN STAR/DIRECTOR: One of you is a porn director giving precise directions while filming your favourite actor pleasuring themselves.

VIRGIN/EXPERIENCED LOVER: Give a primer in the art of sex.

EMPLOYEE/BOSS: The stern boss teaches the employee how to get ahead.

PATIENT/DOCTOR: The medico gets seduced by a horny patient or vice versa.

TEACHER/STUDENT: The teacher punishes a troublemaker student.

COP/THIEF: The cop tells the thief what they can do to get off (literally!).

Game for it

Some sex games are ice breakers, designed to get you going; others are for more deviant fun. The main thing is that your game lets you get into the role playing and using the kinky sex toy without sweating the how-to logistics. You can even let your lover know about your secret fantasy without actually having the dreaded "I'd-really-love-to use a vibrator up your butt/pretend I'm your 'ho'/be tied up" conversation.

Best of all, this is one game you'll never mind losing. Pass the parcel was never this much fun!

You can always use any old game such as Twister, Scrabble or Monopoly and create new sexy rules for it.

RATING
*It'll get you in the mood
**He'll never have to guess how to turn you on again
***You'll be too busy climaxing to finish the game

BUY IT

Oral Sex Dice comes with two dice with endless mouth sex forfeits plus a mini how-to guide. *

The Sex Game board game turns your home into a sexual playground – you'll never know what you have to get up to or where you'll have to do it when you roll the dice. ***

DIY IT

Lucky Dip lets you live out your fantasies – write your top ten on slips of paper, put them in a bowl and then shoot dice to see who gets to dip first.**

Have a Sexy Treasure Hunt by taking turns to secretly write a horny question, a sex request or a sex IOU on each of ten small pieces of paper and then hiding them in different parts of the house. The writer tells the player their prize is near, say, water – it's up to them to find the very explicit piece of paper tucked inside the shower. ***

BUY IT

Adultrivia (played by two or more players) has thousands of lewd informative questions and answers about sex broken into six categories: bawdy jokes, the facts of life, hot times in history, sex in the arts, the famous uncovered, and miscellaneous. *

As you travel around a journey on board of The Kama Sutra Game, you'll travel around each other's bodies and pick up a few tips on what the other finds sexy. * *

52 Weeks Of Naughty Nights is full of sensual thrills, kinky surprises, erotic experiences and playful games – simply pull a card from the silk pouch and scratch off to see what naughty surprise awaits you and your partner. * * *

DIY IT

Gamble with your secrets playing Truth or Dare – ask each other specific sex questions like, "Have you ever had a threesome?" Or, "Have you ever had sex in public?" The other person can either answer truthfully – or they can keep shtum, but take a dare set by you instead (playing doctor dress-up, for example). * *

Play Blind Man's Bluff – one of you puts on a blindfold, the other breaks open the toy chest (you'll need to stock it for this game) and uses various toys on you, one minute per toy. As soon as you guess five toys, it's your turn to play game-master. *

In Lock Up, one person cuffs the other, sets a timer and then, using sex toy of choice, tantalizingly starts to tease their partner. The winner is whoever can beat the timer and bear it the longest. * * *

Glossary

Anal beads/balls: Anal/vaginal beads resemble a cheap plastic necklace. Beads are put into the vagina or anus and then pulled out rapidly during orgasm for ooh-la-la sensation.

Arm binders: Heavy-duty restraints, typically leather, that bind both arms behind the back. Some resemble large gloves that pull up over both arms and buckle around the shoulders. Others are straps that go down the middle of the back and have attached wrist cuffs.

BDSM play: A mixture of bondage and discipline, domination and submission, and sadomasochism.

Ben Wa balls: A pair of plum-sized orbs meant to be inserted into the vagina to rock your world.

Blindfold: An easy way to indulge in a little bondage play – the user gives up their power by going "blind".

Blow-up dolls: Blow-up dolls can come complete with a vagina, rectum, penis, and mouth. "Not tonight, I have a headache," becomes a thing of the past.

Body bags: If you like being bound, the ultimate extreme is bondage which encompasses your entire body, leaving you with no motion whatever. Bondage body bags (or "sleep sacks") resemble a well-tailored, snug sleeping bag, often made out of leather or spandex. Many have openings for genitals or nipples, so your bottom can be pleasured or tortured while you are immobile.

Bondage toys: Gags, blindfolds, and restraints. They are used in erotic power games, where one lover plays dominant (the top), while the other plays submissive (the bottom).

The bottom: The person who relinquishes control in a BDSM (see above) relationship.

Bullet: The bullet is a tiny vibrator that is inserted right into the vagina or anus. It is about the size of a fat thumb.

Butterfly: A vibrator that is designed to be worn against the clitoris, held in place by straps.

Butt plug: This is exactly what it sounds like – a plug for your butt. Anal plugs are often the preferred toys for anal stimulation, because they have a cap at one end that prevents the object from being swallowed up and lost in unknown territory by an over-eager rectum. They are flexible rubber or jelly and range from itty-bitty to mammoth. Using one instead of other objects will ensure that you won't ever have to have a very awkward 3 a.m. conversation with one of the ER nurses.

Clitoral stimulators: These are toys designed to come in direct contact with the clitoris and give it an erotic tickle. There are a variety of clitoral stimulators that are available and they include the strap-on "butterflies", classic dildos or vibrators with extra clitoral nubs and penis rings with clitoral extensions.

Cock ring/erection ring: This is a rubber or metal doughnut-shaped device or leather strap that is placed around the base of the penis (and sometimes, testicles) to give him a firmer handle on his erections (although some men wear them 24/7).

Cyberskin™: An extremely realistic skin-like material used in many sex toys.

Desensitizer: A quick fix if he's a speed shooter or you're getting into some anal play.

Dildo (AKA dong): The best way to explain a dildo, bottom line, is to say that it is a fake solid penis. Dildos come in a dazzling array of styles, shapes and sizes. (They're not all whoppers.) They also come in a variety of materials, including silicone, glass, jelly, and latex. They can be used in sex play or masturbation and can be inserted into the vagina, mouth or anus.

Double dildo: Double the pleasure, double the fun of the single variety, this model has two penis-like heads so they can be used by two people.

Extenders/PPAs: Imagine a condom with a three-inch dildo on the end. Extenders elongate the erect penis, allowing deeper insertion.

Female pumps: Don't get your hopes up – this has nothing to do with boosting breast growth. Also known as clitoris and/or breast pumps, these toys come with a suction cup that is either placed over the clitoral area or the nipple. Once a grip has been established, a vibrating stimulator is turned on sending pulsating vibes to the designated area.

Fetish wear: Think black, think leather. Sexy lingerie usually used in S&M or bondage play.

Flogger: This is similar to a whip; however, it has more than one strand of leather on the end of it so the area being touched is wider.

French tickler: Basically, a condom with tiny nubs on it which can be used to give added stimulation to the entire vaginal region during sex. They're usually not certified for birth control or disease prevention.

G-spot stimulator: Dildo or vibrator that has a bent come-hither tip which, when placed in the vagina, arouses the G-spot.

Gag: Made from leather or cloth, gags are used to fill the mouth. This eliminates talking, but not sounds of sexual pleasure. Used for BDSM play.

Harness: A plastic or leather device worn around the hips and pelvis which then holds a strap-on dildo or butt plug in place. Can be used by men or women.

Hobble skirts: One for the fetishists. These are leather or rubber skirts which fit very snugly from waist down to ankles. Often the wearer can take steps of only a few inches while wearing the skirt (thus the term "hobble skirt"). When combined with a pair of high heels, these skirts can be almost totally immobilizing, even without any other bondage.

Hoods: Leather or rubber covering for the head used in BDSM. Some hoods have mouth holes, some don't. Some deluxe hoods have built-in earmuffs or even space for earphones, for sensory deprivation. Almost all hoods have nose holes, for obvious reasons.

Jelly: A rubbery material used in the manufacture of some sex toys. It has the texture of gummy candies.

Latex: The rubbery plastic commonly used in the manufacture of sex toys.

Lubricants: Emollients (oils, lotions, and creams) that, when applied to the skin or to a sex toy, can increases its slipperiness, making sex a more comfortable affair.

Mask: A face covering which is worn to heighten erotic excitement in S&M and bondage play. Made of cloth or leather (see Hood).

Massage oils: Scented lotions and oils that are used in during erotic massages (or therapeutic ones) and add to sensual play.

Massager: What vibrators used to be called. Sold primarily to promote muscle massage, however, their uses are far more popular in sexual play.

Masturbator: These can also be called a "sleeve" or "penis sleeves". Masturbators are sex toys used by men to give them a taste of the real thing during masturbation. Most are crafted to look like vaginas (in which case, they are called "sleeves"), and a vibrator in the toy adds variation.

Mummification or cocooning: About the most complete form of bondage. A person is wrapped up, usually with cling film limb by limb, so they are completely immobile.

Nipple clamps/nipple clips: Nipple toys can be worn and enjoyed by both women and men. They're often attached with a chain.

PC muscle (AKA pubococcygeus muscle): This is actually a sling of muscles that support the pelvic floor and encircle the genitals of both sexes. Exercise it and you may experience stronger and more intense orgasms.

Penis pump: A mechanical device that creates a vacuum-like suction around the penis. This temporarily coaxes more blood into the organ, resulting in a somewhat larger, firmer erection.

Penis sleeve: See Masturbator. PPAS (Penile Projection Assistants): Supposedly, the quickest way to turn a 10cm (four inch) willy into a 25cm (10 inch) monster. They slide over the dick and keep it hard. For those nights when Viagra just doesn't cut it.

Realistic: Sex toys that are moulded from an actual penis or vagina, usually a professional's (this is the closest you'll probably ever get to having sex with a porn star).

Restraints: Any device such as ropes, silk scarves, handcuffs and ribbons that are used for bondage sexual play.

Riding crop: A small equestrian whip used in sexual power play.

STIs (sexually transmitted infections): any disease that's transmitted during sexual intercourse (anal, oral or vaginal). Such diseases include AIDS (HIV), chlamydia, genital herpes, genital warts (HPV), gonorrhea, hepatitis B, crab lice, syphilis and trichomoniasis.

Sexual aid (AKA Sex toy): A catch-all term for any device used for sexual stimulation.

Silicone: The cashmere of sex toy materials, it's nonporous, has great texture, can be moulded in stunning detail, is hypoallergenic and retains body heat.

Strap-on: A dildo or butt plug inserted into a plastic or leather harness to wear on your hips, thigh, pelvis, chest or even your face to penetrate a partner. The strap-on can allow more realistic intercourse than hand-held toys. Can be used by both men and women.

Swing: The swing hangs from a high-strength spring and rotating eyebolt (usually included), from the ceiling which allows the users an incredible range of new and exciting sexual positions. The seat, back and stirrups are padded for your comfort, and the instruction manual suggests many sensual positions.

Titilizer: Sexy breast jewellery that loops around the nipples and plays up the wearer's cup size.

Tongue: This is a vibrator shaped like an extended human tongue (yes, you read right) and can it ever move like one! Best of all, it's mute. So you get all of the oral action with no aural strain. Moving at variable speeds it allows the user to get vaginal, clitoral or anal stimulation.

The top: The person who takes control in a BDSM (see above) relationship.

Vaginal simulator: See Masturbator.

Vibrator: The name pretty much says it all. What we're dealing with here is a toy that vibrates, often with varying speeds, and when used on the clitoris is one of the easiest ways for a woman to reach orgasm. Vibrators sometimes resemble gyrating dildos and can be used anally or vaginally. Some have an attachment for simultaneous clitoral stimulation, such as the "Rabbit" featured on *Sex and the City* (the latter is the type enthusiastically endorsed for those of you who have a clitoris). For the shopper who might prefer "friendlier-looking" toys, there are vibrators that look like lipsticks, butterflies and even seashells.

Whip: General term used for a toy that when used strikes a person adding erotic sensations. See Floggers, Riding Crops.

Resources

You can get virtually anything and everything you need in the way of sex toy equipment – supplies, advice, good reads, X-rated films, hand-holding, information and so on – from your friendly on-line sex boutique.

SEX BOUTIQUES

A quick guide to some of the more tasteful,discriminating, friendly sex toy shops on the Internet. In general, you'll get a higher quality of products, helpful sex information, realistic product reviews, and special emphasis on women and couples.

Ann Summers: Stores throughout the UK plus a website. Also a source for hosting sex toy parties.
Customer care telephone: 0845 456 2320 (8am-5.30pm, Monday–Wednesday, Friday; 9.30am–5.30pm Thursday).
Website: www.annsummers.com

Blowfish: This site has more of a hip edge to it – lots of frank talk, toys that run the sexual gamut, and a witty, humorous writing style. (Great if you get tired of women's sites that can be relentlessly wholesome!). Good selection of toys, books, and videos.
Website: www.blowfish.com

Good Vibrations: One of the original women-owned sex toy companies, this site boasts a good selection of well-reviewed toys, books and videos, along with a magazine and the must-see antique vibrator museum. Retail stores in San Francisco and Berkeley, California.
Website: www.goodvibrations.com

Libida: This on-line store is geared toward women and couples. The site features a good range of toys, books, and videos reviewed by its female staff, plus some great how-tos, sexy horoscopes, topical articles, and a "decision-maker" designed to help you choose a product.
Website: www.libida.com

LoveHoney: A wide selection of on-line goodies.
Address: Unit 6, 3 Edgar Buildings, George Street, Bath, Somerset BA1 2FJ. Freephone: 0800 915 6635
Monday–Friday 8am–9pm; Saturday–Sunday 9am–5pm.
Website: www.lovehoney.co.uk

Natural Instinct: sells funky designer sex toys plus a wide selection of your more conventional stuff.
Address: 75 Poets Chase, Aylesbury HP21 7LP.
Phone: 0870 794 2130.
Website: www.naturalinstinct.co.uk

Sh!: A women-friendly shop run by women.
Address: 39 Coronet Street, London N1 6HD.
Phone: 0207 613 5458 (Monday–Friday).
Website: www.sh-womenstore.com

Vixen Creations: A woman-owned hand-made dildo manufacturer, this outfit makes some of the highest quality silicone dildos on the market. They wholesale to sex toy retailers, but offer a good chunk of their product line direct to consumers on their web site.
Website: www.vixencreations.com

Xandria: One of the first companies to cater to a couples' market, Xandria's got an extensive product line (toys mostly), but the reviews can feel a little overhyped. "Shop by Benefit" is one of the nicer features – you can see the products that appeal to certain groups (gay men or women, hard to find sizes, etc).
Website: www.xandria.com

GOOD READS

Some titillating tomes to curl up with:

ESO: How You and Your Lover Can Give Each Other Hours of Extended Sexual Orgasm, by Alan P. Brauer and Donna Brauer, will teach you how to use genital massage to master living in an hours-long orgasmic state.

Herotica for Women, by Susie Bright, published by Down There Press. A series of erotic fiction collections for women. There are currently six volumes in the series.

Sex for One: The Joy of Self-Loving, by Betty Dodson, tells you all you need to know about letting your fingers do the walking.

The Tao of Sexual Massage, by Stephen Russell and Jurgen Kolb, will turn you into a sex-goddess masseuse.

Any book on sex fantasies (check out Nancy Friday's series) or *Hot Sex Fantasies*, by yours truly.

SEXY VIDEOS

Learn a trick or two from these sexy flicks.

Erotic Seduction: Sex Toys (available from www.lovingsex.com or www.yoursexcoach.com) with adult star Juli Ashton offers educational tips on the wide range of sex toys, with entertaining, explicit scenes to demonstrate their use.

The Complete Guide to Sex Toys and Devices (available from www.yoursexcoach.com) has couples demonstrating an incredible and delectable range of options for their mutual pleasuring.

Any of Candida Royalle's videos (available from www.royalle.com) are made with women in mind – in other words, no money shot of ejaculation spurting all over the place and lots of steamy seductive scenes.

HOT WEBSITES

Log onto www.nerve.com for smart, interesting, titillating, frank sex stories, articles and essays.

Index

Picture Credits

The publishers would like to thank the following sources for their kind permission to reproduce the pictures in this book. The page numbers for each of the photographs are listed below, giving the page on which they appear in the book and any location indicator (c-centre, t-top, b-bottom, l-left, r-right)